NA

551.5

D1342693

Items should be ~~returned on or before the last~~ date
shown below. Items not already requested by other
borrowers may be renewed in person, in writing or by
telephone. To renew, please quote the number on the
barcode label. To renew online a PIN is required.
This can be requested at your local library.
Renew online @ **www.dublincitypubliclibraries.ie**
Fines charged for overdue items will include postage
incurred in recovery. Damage to or loss of items will
be charged to the borrower.

Leabharlanna Poiblí Chathair Bhaile Átha Cliath
Dublin City Public Libraries

Dublin City
Baile Átha Cliath

Date Due	Date Due	Date Due
23. MAR 09	01. NOV 14	
15. DEC 10	13 MAR 2017	10. FEB 18.
02. SEP 14.	28 MAR 2018	

THE BOOK OF
WEATHER EYE

THE BOOK OF WEATHER EYE

An Anthology, compiled by Anne McWilliams

BRENDAN McWILLIAMS ∿

Gill & Macmillan

Gill & Macmillan Ltd
Hume Avenue, Park West, Dublin 12
with associated companies throughout the world
www.gillmacmillan.ie

© The late Brendan McWilliams 2008
978 07171 4581 2

Typography design by Make Communication
Print origination by Carole Lynch
Printed and bound in the UK by CPI Mackays, Chatham ME5 8TD

This book is typeset in Linotype Minion and
Neue Helvetica.

The paper used in this book comes from the wood pulp of
managed forests. For every tree felled, at least one tree is
planted, thereby renewing natural resources.

A CIP catalogue record for this book is available from the
British Library.

5 4 3

Dedication

For my darling Brendan
as I promised

FOREWORD

A Weather Eye on My Father

> *The original writer is not the one who*
> *refrains from imitating others, but one who*
> *can be imitated by none.*
> François René Chateaubriand

If few popular writers succeed in carving such a niche for themselves that they become irreplaceable, then Brendan McWilliams was surely the exception. His daily *Weather Eye* column, which ran in *The Irish Times* for almost twenty years, conveyed eloquently the popular aspects of meteorology, climate, astronomy and the environment. Easy to digest, and sprinkled lightly with literature, history, folklore and mischievous humour, it was often the first article to which readers turned each morning.

This book represents a labour of love for my mother, Anne. Containing some of the best examples of *Weather Eye*, it is a collection of pieces from 2006—a period when my father was, perhaps, at his creative peak. In response to the numerous letters and emails he received almost daily from readers requesting another book, he was in the process of preparing *A Weather Eye on Weather Lore* and had further plans for *A Weather Eye on History*. Alas, these projects were hardly underway when he learned suddenly of his illness, and was obliged by his doctors to take some rest. Sadly, Dad passed away a few weeks later, on 22 October 2007.

But let us go back to the beginning. Brendan McWilliams was born on 7 August 1944 and grew up in Waterville, Co. Kerry, where his father, Seán, was the meteorologist in charge of the nearby Valentia Observatory. My father graduated in science from University College Cork in 1964, and later in Business Administration from University

College Dublin. He worked as a meteorologist throughout his adult life and, during the 1970s, was well known as a presenter of the daily weather forecast on RTÉ radio and television. For much of the 1990s, he was Assistant Director of Met Éireann, and a frequent Delegate of Ireland at meetings of numerous bodies concerned with international co-operation in meteorology. Finally, from 1998 until his retirement in 2004, he was Director of Administration and a member of the Management Board of the European Meteorological Satellite Organisation (EUMETSAT) in Germany.

Amidst all this, the *Weather Eye* column began quietly on 9 August 1988. Dad composed his earliest offerings on an ancient Olivetti typewriter, often churning out half-a-dozen drafts that my mother would diligently edit, until a finished manuscript was finally arrived upon. This was a daily routine, each piece generally written thirty-six hours in advance and delivered the following morning on his way to work. Monday's article was the only exception, because Dad did not travel to work on Sundays. I was dispatched instead, a mere lad of fourteen, bus fare in one hand and envelope in the other, ready to deliver my precious cargo to the Duty Chief Sub-Editor at the *Irish Times* offices in Fleet Street.

The old mechanical typewriter was eventually replaced by an electric one, and then by a painfully slow Amstrad computer that seemed to run on coal. But it was not until the arrival of email that I was spared my Sunday afternoon trips into town. Later, during Dad's time in Germany, each of the numerous business trips or holidays around Europe would be marked first by the search for a local internet café so that the article might be emailed each afternoon without hindrance. Indeed, in over nineteen years of writing, he never once missed a deadline, and was proud to call *Weather Eye* the longest-running daily column in an Irish newspaper by a single author until its final instalment on 3 October 2007.

But to those of us who knew him best, the so-called 'Clerk of the Weather' seemed to lead a kind of double life. Far from being a public figure, he was our Dad: a family man, warm and wise; a voracious and curious reader, often with several books on the go at once. He had a wonderfully dry and irreverent sense of humour and a real grasp of irony. With a single well-placed remark or a subtle statement of the obvious, he made the ordinary seem suddenly absurd, exposed for what it truly was. There was always laughter in our house.

Dad, of course, loved Shakespeare. As children, when sending us off to bed, he would quote from *Hamlet* as he bid us, '…Good night, sweet prince, and flights of angels sing thee to thy rest!' His passion for literature and history can be felt at the turn of almost every page in this book. Similarly, his concern for the environment is evident, as is his desire to impart what he saw as the inevitable truth about global warming. He was fastidious in his research, regarding himself as a 'magpie' who would ferret out and collect serendipitous pieces of information before weaving them into something useful. He relied upon his readers and Met Service colleagues to help him in this task, and was continuously grateful to those who wrote to him with helpful suggestions.

His achievements were many. He was awarded, in 1999, Honorary Life Membership of the Royal Dublin Society and, in 2005, Honorary Membership of the Irish Meteorological Society. But he remained, throughout, a modest figure, a true gentleman who lived—as he wrote— with great warmth and lightness of touch. Some of his best work is captured within this volume; something for everyone, perhaps, from Napoleon's restoration of the Gregorian calendar to the search for sea level. What a truly original writer. I am proud to have called him Father.

Stephen McWilliams
July 2008

THE END OF A REVOLUTIONARY IDEAL

2 January 2006 ~

'*L*e calendrier gregorien sera mis en usage dans tout l'Empire francais.' Napoleon's proclamation restoring the Gregorian Calendar to official use throughout the French Empire came into effect 200 years ago yesterday, on 1 January 1806. It brought to an end what was, literally, a Revolutionary experiment in chronology, and one which was not without its merits.

With the establishment of the Republic in 1792, the entire French administrative infrastructure was carefully reviewed. As part of this, the Academy of Sciences was ordered to produce a suitable French alternative to the traditional Gregorian way of reckoning the months and years, and so it was that a new Republican Calendar was unveiled the following year.

The twelve months of the new Calendar were uniformly 30 days in length, and were given names according to a system devised by the poet Philippe Fabre d'Eglantine, intended to reflect the French climate and the cycle of its agricultural year. Thus 'Rain' or *pluviose* occurred in what had once been January, *germinal* or 'Seed-Time' began in March, and *thermidor* occurred during the sultry days that coincided with the height of summer. The months were distinguished according to season by their suffixes, the autumn months ending in *-aire*, the winter ones in *-ose*, the spring in *-al*, and the summer months in *-dor*.

Since the twelve months together amounted to only 360 days, the extra five or six required to keep in step with Nature were added here and there, and designated as festivals or public holidays. In addition, the seven-day week was abandoned, and each month was divided into three *decades*, with the last day of each decade being a rest day.

New Year's Day was to be at the autumn equinox. Moreover, it was decided that the new arrangements should be back-dated to 22 September 1792, which not only saw the beginning of the new Republic, but had also been, by coincidence, the autumn equinox in that particular year.

The Republican Calendar was remarkably accurate in its construction. Its year had an average length of 365.24225 days, a difference of only five days in 100,000 years, compared to what we now know to be the proper figure. And the names devised by Fabre d'Eglantine were both attractive and ingenious, even if the zone in which they could be used with their intended logic was geographically limited.

But despite its accuracy and many elements of common sense, France's new Calendar never quite caught on. It was widely used during its official 13 years in force for conducting the affairs of State, but your average tumbrel-driver on the Rue St Jacques was not impressed and the ordinary people found it hard to change from the Gregorian system to which they had been long accustomed. Perhaps the most frequently heard complaint was that with the Republican Calendar they now had only one day off in ten—instead of one in seven.

SKIES OF BLUE—AND BLACK AND WHITE

4 January 2006 ∾

'**D**ear Brendan,' wrote a correspondent recently, 'I read with much interest your article on the colours of the Moon, and towards the end you explain why the day-time Moon appears white because of the blue influence of the sky. But why is the sky blue?' The question has been addressed, of course, several times in *Weather Eye* before, but for completeness' sake, let us recap.

Light, as we know, is a wave motion. And if you watch waves moving along the surface of a body of water, you will notice that an obstruction of an appropriate size—a rock, for instance—disrupts the original wave train, and sends other sets of wavelets off in various directions. Light waves are affected in the same way by the tiny molecules of our atmosphere, by a process known as *scattering*.

Now light acquires its colour from its wavelength. Blue light, for example, has a very short wavelength, while the wavelength of red light is relatively long; the 'white' light from the Sun is a mixture of all the colours of the spectrum from blue, through yellow, green and orange, to red. As it happens, the molecules of air in our atmosphere are of such a size that they scatter the very short wavelengths of blue light much more efficiently than they do the longer ones of the other colours. A *little* of the red and orange is scattered, for example, but the proportion is small compared to the amount of blue.

When you look at a part of the sky away from the Sun, you see sunlight which was originally heading in an entirely different direction, but which has been scattered towards you by the atmosphere.

And since, by and large, only the very short blue waves are affected in this way, you see the scattered light—and therefore most of the sky—as blue.

Near the horizon, matters are more complex. At this very shallow angle the sunlight scattered in our direction approaches us almost horizontally through the air and must travel a much longer path than usual before it reaches us. Because of this long distance, the scattered blue light is subject to further attenuation on its journey by the atmosphere; it is 're-scattered' before it reaches our eyes, and much of it is, therefore, extinguished. But the small amounts of orange and red light which were originally scattered in our direction are likely to survive this long journey with little further interference. In this way, the balanced proportions required to produce white light are virtually restored, so near the horizon, looking away from the Sun, the sky is as near to white as makes no difference.

If, on the other hand, our planet had no atmosphere to scatter light, the Sun would appear as pure white, and all the rest of the sky would be a dark and inky black.

THE PREVIEW OF 2006 IS NOW COMPLETE

5 January 2006 ∿

'This night makes an end wholly of Christmas,' recorded Samuel Pepys in his diary, 'with a mind fully satisfied with the great pleasures we have had. And it is high time to betake myself to my late vows, that I may for a great while do my duty and increase my good name and esteem in the world, and get money which sweetens all things and whereof I have much need.' And then, even if he had not told us so explicitly, we have a clue as to which the night might be: 'After dinner to the Duke's house, and there saw *Twelfth Night* acted well, though it be but a silly play and not relating at all to the name or day.'

It is strange to think of William Shakespeare at a loss for a title for a play, but that allegedly was the case on this occasion. The name, as Pepys noted, has nothing whatever to do with the convoluted contents of the play itself, but recalls the fact that it was written to be performed for the first time at the Twelfth Night revelries, probably those of January 1601.

Twelfth Night is tonight, the eve of Old Christmas Day, or the night before *Nollaig na mBan* as it was called in Ireland, the day on which women had the traditional privilege of resting from their housework. Its significance stems partly from the old Julian Calendar used in these parts until 1752, by which Christmas Day fell on the day we now designate the 6th of January. Twelfth Night in former times was an occasion for great merry-making. Whoever found the bean in the Twelfth Night cake became the Bean King, and set the tone for the festivities; at the end of the party all decorations were taken down, and the holly and ivy were carefully stowed away to be used to start the fire on which the pancakes would be made on Shrove Tuesday.

It was also believed that a sneak preview of the weather for the coming year could be obtained easily by keeping a close eye on conditions 'between Christmas and the Kings'. The idea was that the Twelve Days of Christmas were 'days of fate', each symbolically governing the character of the month that occupies the corresponding place for the succeeding year.

'What the weather shall be on the sixth and twentieth day of December,' wrote Gervase Markham—who, coincidentally, was a

contemporary of Shakespeare and one of that select band of talented writers who are sometimes suspected of having written
many of the plays—'the like shall it be in the month of January;
what it shall be on the seventh and twentieth, the like shall be the
following February; and so on until the Twelfth Day, each day's
weather foreshowing a month of the year.'

LIVING IN FEAR OF THE WHITE DEATH

6 January 2006 ∾

Robert Browning, as far as I know, never visited America.
Yet one of his better known poems, 'Prospice', is remarkably prescient of a meteorological phenomenon prevalent
at this time of year in western parts of the United States. You will
remember the little verse from school:

> *Fear death?—to feel the fog in my throat,*
>   *The mist in my face,*
> *When the snows begin, and the blasts denote*
>   *I am nearing the place.*

Down the centuries, fog has always had a sinister reputation.
Mediaeval fogs were dreaded as the embodiment of an unhealthy
dampness, as catalysts for rheumatic aches and pains, and as evil
vectors for every kind of ague and fever. Nor indeed were these
fears always without foundation; during the London fog which

began on 5 December 1952, and lasted several weeks, the death rate more than doubled and it was reckoned that, allowing for 'normal' mortality, the foggy spell had claimed 4,000 people's lives.

The *pogonip* was feared for similar reasons, and indeed its very name has lethal connotations, deriving as it does from the language of the Shoshone Indians in which the word 'pogonip'—or *pakenappeh*—means 'white death'. A report in the *American Meteorological Journal* in 1887, for example, has it that 'To breathe the pogonip is death to the lungs, and when it comes, the people rush for cover. When it ascends from the valleys its chill embrace is so much feared by the Indians, who are predisposed to infections of the lungs, that they change their camp if apprised by the atmospheric conditions that the dreaded fog is imminent.'

When fog exists at sub-zero temperatures, a white crystalline deposit known as rime may be seen to build up on the windward side of obstacles like shrubs or garden fences. This 'freezing fog', which we see occasionally in Ireland, is composed of water droplets that are 'supercooled', continuing to exist in the liquid state at temperatures well below the normal freezing point of water. A supercooled water droplet, however, quickly freezes when it comes into contact with a solid object.

Sometimes, however, when the temperature is very low indeed, excess water vapour in the atmosphere condenses directly into ice crystals rather than into tiny droplets of water. This is the pogonip, common in wintertime in the vicinity of the Sierra Nevada Mountains. As with rime, ice crystals drifting in the air adhere to trees and fences, often forming spectacular patterns; some say the colliding crystals can be heard to tinkle in the air as they jostle gently with each other.

We know now, however, that unlike the London fogs, the pogonip is harmless. It is likely that its sinister reputation arose from the prevalence of tuberculosis in the late nineteenth century, and the fact that breathing harsh, cold air, whether containing little particles of ice or not, probably exacerbates existing conditions of the lungs.

WHEN NO BIRDS SING

7 January 2006 ∾

We are at the time of year when

> . . . *yellow leaves, or none, or few, do hang*
> *Upon those boughs which shake against the cold,*
> *Bare ruin'd choirs, where late the sweet birds sang.*

Some birds are still here, of course, flitting aimlessly from ruined choir to shaking bough, but Shakespeare is right: the *joie de vivre* is gone and no bird sings; all huddle silently together along the very base of Maslow's famous triangle.

Many have simply gone away, but it has not always been clear precisely where they went. The sixteenth-century Archbishop Olaus Magnus of Uppsala had the theory that swallows, for example, descend first into the reeds in autumn 'and thence into the waters below them, bound mouth to mouth, wing to wing, and foot to foot'. Fishermen, it was said, might often draw up a lumpy mass of these coagulated birds, and if the lump were warmed, the swallows would revive and start their summer antics a month or two too soon.

Giraldus Cambrensis, too, a frequent visitor to Ireland in the twelfth century, seemed to hint in his *Topographia Hiberniae* at a similar notion as to how birds might survive the rigours of winter: 'It is remarkable', he wrote, 'about birds that are accustomed to disappear during the winter that in the interval, neither dead nor alive, they seem to continue living in their vital spirit and at the same time to be seized up into a long ecstasy and some middle state between life and death.'

The local availability of food is the main criterion determining where individuals spend their winter. Birds like the swallow who feed almost entirely on the wing have no choice but to migrate southwards when the chilly autumn weather brings a dearth of airborne insects. Farther north, wading birds and waterfowl, imperilled by freezing water, are obliged to make their way southwards to our more temperate shores. Other species, which depend on convective air currents induced by solar warmth to keep them aloft while hunting, move southwards when lower temperatures remove any liveliness the air might have.

Those birds remaining must survive on whatever food they find. Some depend on seeds and berries, while scavengers like gulls and crows eat anything from discarded household waste to crops unharvested in fields, or other animals killed upon the roads. And all must survive the bitter, winter cold.

The riskiness of a non-migratory strategy is inherent in the fact that resident songbirds tend to produce several broods a year, each containing as many as a dozen eggs; migratory species, by contrast, in general lay fewer eggs and breed but once. The reason for the difference is assumed to be that the resident species have a higher mortality rate in winter than that experienced by their travelling cousins, even taking into account the lengthy, hazardous journeys undertaken by the latter.

THE PREDICTIONS OF AN UGLY FORECASTER

9 January 2006 ∿

Today's forecasters conjure up predictions from their weather maps, or furtively extract the future from computer print-outs. In times gone by, however, such predictive skills were sometimes quite innate. Mother Shipton, for example, specialised in very long-range forecasts and in many spheres her record seems impressive.

She was born Ursula Sontheil in 1488, her arrival in this world, it is said, having come about as a result of a brief dalliance between her teenage mother and the Prince of Darkness on a stormy night. It was stormy, too, on the day that she was born, but it is recorded that 'the tempest could not affright the women more than the prodigious physiognomy of the child; the body was long but very big-boned; she had great gobbling eyes, very sharp and fiery, and a nose of unproportionable length, having in it many crooks and turnings adorned with great pimples'.

Be that as it may, young Ursula grew up to be a strange, unworldly creature, who lived for 80 years or thereabouts in her native town of Knaresborough in Yorkshire. In 1512 she married a carpenter called Toby Shipton, who appears to have contributed nothing more to history than to provide his wife with the name by which we know her now. Mother Shipton became famous even in her lifetime for her prophecies, and she recorded her visions of the future in iambic verse.

She was remarkably percipient about the future of technology, particularly for one writing in the early sixteenth century. She has proved to be equally accurate, for example, on such widely diverse topics as ladies' fashions, combine harvesters, films, aeroplanes and submarines:

> *For in those wondrous far off days,*
> *The women shall adopt a craze*
> *To dress like men, and trousers wear,*
> *And to cut off their locks of hair;*
> *And roaring monsters, with men atop,*
> *Shall seem to eat the verdant crop.*
> *And men shall fly as birds do now,*
> *And give away the horse and plough.*
> *Pictures shall come alive with movements free,*
> *And boats, like fishes, swim beneath the sea.*

So perhaps we ought to listen to what Mother Shipton has to say on climate matters:

> *The tides will rise beyond their ken*
> *To bite away the shores, and then,*
> *The flooding waters rushing in,*
> *Will flood the lands with such a din*
> *That mankind cowers in muddy fen*
> *And snarls about his fellow men.*
> *Not every land on earth will sink;*
> *Those that do not will stench and stink*
> *Of rotting bodies of beast and man,*
> *And vegetation crisped on land.*

Could this be a cautionary insight into the consequences of unmitigated greenhouse warming?

TWO CENTURIES OF THE BEAUFORT SCALE

13 January 2006 ∾

Two hundred years ago today, on the morning of 13 January 1806, the three-masted frigate HMS *Woolwich* sailed with the tide from the Isle of Wight, bound for the West Indies. Her captain, 32-year-old Commander Francis Beaufort from Navan, County Meath, dined alone in his cabin that evening and afterwards wrote up his journal: 'Hereafter I shall estimate the force of the wind according to the following scale, since nothing can convey a more uncertain idea of the wind than the old expressions of moderate and stiff, etc., etc.' This initiative was to bring him worldwide and permanent recognition in far greater measure than any heroic sea battle in which he might ever have been engaged.

Beaufort enumerated 14 wind forces, from zero to 13, in a list which closely resembles the Beaufort Scale we use today. But the idea in this form was not original; his scale was only a slight variation of one devised in 1779 by Alexander Dalrymple of the East India Company, who had in turn borrowed an idea proposed to the Royal Society in 1759 by the engineer John Smeaton in a paper on windmills.

In 1810, however, Beaufort, now commander of the *Blossom*, added his personal stamp to what was to become the Beaufort Scale. He refined it to 13 forces, and included for each a description of how much canvas the typical full-rigged man-o'-war could comfortably carry. A *light air*, Force 1, for example, was a wind just sufficient 'to give steering way'; a *moderate breeze*, Force 2, was a wind such that a 'well-conditioned man-o'-war, under all sail . . . would go in smooth water at from 5 to 6 knots'; with Force 8, a *whole gale*, the same ship could only bear 'close-reefed main topsails and a reefed foresail'; and the highest number, *hurricane*, Force 12, was when a man-o'-war could show no canvas whatsoever.

With this arrangement, Beaufort had gone far beyond the scale he had copied from Dalrymple four years earlier, assessing the wind against a well-known standard in much the same way as a standard unit might be used to determine an object's length. Its great functional advantage was that it measured the *force* of the wind, and not its speed; at that time it was impossible to measure wind speed at sea with any accuracy, but using the concept of force, all trained observers could arrive at the same number on the scale merely by glancing at the sails and gauging the performance of their vessel.

By 1834, Captain Beaufort was Hydrographer to the Navy, and was able to instruct all his surveyors to use the scale he had devised. Four years later it was adopted for general use throughout the British Navy, and by the time he died in 1857, Admiral Sir Francis Beaufort's Scale of Wind Force was used by mariners in every corner of the world.

CARELESS HABITS OF ACCURACY

14 *January* 2006 ∼

Weatherpeople often trouble themselves about things of little concern to ordinary mortals. A few years ago, for example, a topic of the hour was whether on the previous day a certain individual had 'forecasted' the weather, or merely 'forecast' it. Naturally enough, recourse was had to Henry Watson Fowler's *Modern English Usage*, a *vade mecum* no decent weather office is without.

'Whether we are to say *forecast* or *forecasted* in the past tense and participle', says Henry Watson, 'depends on whether we regard the verb or the noun as the original from which the other is formed; if the verb is original (meaning to guess beforehand) the past and present participle will be *cast*. . .; if the verb is derived (meaning to make a forecast) they will as certainly be *forecasted*. The verb is in fact recorded 150 years earlier than the noun, and so we may therefore thankfully rid ourselves of the ugly *forecasted*; it may be hoped that we should do so even if history were against us, but this time it is kind.'

The basis for Fowler's conclusion, however, becomes fuzzier when other sources are consulted. The Oxford Dictionary, I am told, informs us with remarkable precision that the word *forecast* has been in use with the special meaning of weather prediction since the year 1673. *The Meteorological Glossary*, on the other hand, says that in 1860 Admiral FitzRoy 'invented the special meaning of the term *forecast* to avoid the somewhat unfortunate connotations attaching to such terms as *prognostic* and *prophecy*'.

Some people, of course, regard such activity as nonsense anyway. 'Of all the silly, irritating foolishness by which we are plagued,' declares Jerome K. Jerome in *Three Men in a Boat*, 'this weather forecasting fraud is about the most aggravating [*sic*]. It forecasts precisely what happened yesterday or the day before, and precisely the opposite of what is going to happen today.'

There is no truth whatever in this grossly unjust, imputed methodology. A forecaster in doubt about tomorrow's weather would never predict simply a repeat of what had been experienced yesterday; he would use the honourable ploy of 'hedging'. David Lodge has its measure when he tells us in his novel *Changing Places* about a radio forecaster who 'predicted every possible combination of temperatures over the next 24 hours without actually committing himself to anything specific, not even the existing temperature'.

An example of hedging might be this: 'Scattered heavy showers or outbreaks of rain today, with long sunny spells in some places; light to moderate variable winds, locally fresh or strong; temperatures near average, with visibility moderate to good, but poor locally in haze or fog. Outlook: little change.' As a technique it owes more to James Joyce than Jerome K. Jerome: 'I've put in so many enigmas and puzzles', gloated the former about *Ulysses*, 'that it will keep the professors busy for centuries over what I meant.'

CELEBRATING THE RAINY WEATHER

16 January 2006 ∿

P ersons with an urge to celebrate often attach little triangles of cloth or plastic in a variety of different colours to a length of string, and then display their handiwork as a sign of their euphoria. They call it bunting. But if you look up the word in almost any dictionary you will find it labelled 'etym. unknown', meaning that no one knows exactly where it came from.

Strangely enough, if you consult instead a German dictionary, you will find that *bunt* means 'many-coloured', 'variegated', 'motley', even 'gay'. Every Easter, for example, the Germans like to paint their breakfast eggs in a wide variety of different colours, and call them *bunte Eier*. It all lends credence, I suppose, to Antoine de Rivarol's famous epigram: *Ce qui n'est pas clair n'est pas français*—'What is not clear is not French.' Indeed! It may be German.

Meteorologists, whether or not in celebratory mood, like to display bunting on their weather maps. If you look at their portrayal of a typical depression, you will notice, trailing southwards from the centre, two bold curved lines tastefully adorned with little pennants, just like bunting; these are fronts. Leading the way is the warm front, with red semi-circular markings; the cold front, with blue pointed barbs, trails behind to form the western boundary of a triangular zone between the two, its apex pointing towards the centre of the low. This area between the fronts is called the 'warm sector', in which the air is usually warmer and more humid than elsewhere.

As a low moves eastwards, its fronts are carried with it and swept anti-clockwise around its centre by the spiralling winds. Both warm and cold fronts may be thought of as elongated zones of rain moving steadily across the surface of the globe from west to east, but each has its own generic character.

The rain associated with a warm front sets in gradually, its approach being signalled first by 'mares' tails', and then by a gradually thickening veil of cirrus cloud. As time goes by the blanket of cloud becomes thicker and lower until at first gentle, and then steadier, rain begins to fall. But when the warm front has passed a particular spot, there is seldom a dramatic change; there follows rather a gradual transition to damp, cloudy, drizzly weather which lasts until the arrival of the second front.

A cold front is more vigorous. Its arrival is often marked by a relatively quick transition from the drizzly warm sector conditions to very heavy, perhaps thundery, rain. Now comes the heaviest downpour of the rainy interlude, but its end is sudden. While the rain still falls, a patch of blue may appear somewhere in the western sky; the rain stops, the Sun breaks through, and the wet glistening countryside takes on a new look of brightness and of life. The cold front has passed by.

A SCIENTIFIC AMERICAN

17 *January* 2006 ∽

Few individuals are sufficiently talented in their chosen field for their name to be remembered centuries later. It is even more exceptional to achieve lasting fame in a number of diverse disciplines, but such a man was Benjamin Franklin—statesman, writer, inventor and, in no small measure, meteorologist.

A printer by trade, Franklin was born in Boston 300 years ago today, on 17 January 1706. He became sufficiently prosperous early in life to be able to devote much of his time to scientific studies and to public service. This financial security was attributable to the phenomenal success of *Poor Richard's Almanac* which Franklin published in Philadelphia for many years and into which, along with all the data usually found in almanacs, he put many of his own ideas and proverbs.

During the 1740s Franklin became interested in the phenomenon of electricity, a subject then very much in vogue, and was convinced that the lightning flashes associated with a thunderstorm were electrical in origin. In 1753 he carried out his famous experiment with a kite to demonstrate, dangerously but conclusively, that this indeed was so, and it was but a small step from this knowledge to the development of 'Franklin rods', or lightning conductors as we call them nowadays, to protect tall structures from a lightning strike.

Among his other legacies is what is probably the first scientific reference to the Gulf Stream. In October 1769, in a letter to the Secretary of the British Post Office, Franklin wrote about 'the Gulph Stream, a strong current which comes out of the Gulph of Florida, running at a rate of three or four miles an hour', and went on to describe its likely effect on the packet steamers carrying mail between Europe and America.

Benjamin Franklin visited Ireland in October 1771, and attended the House of Commons in Dublin, no doubt observing its proceedings closely as a possible model for a legislative assembly for the future United States of America. In due course he became one of the principal spokesmen for the American colonists in their negotiations with the King's ministers and was a signatory of the Declaration of Independence on 4 July 1776. It was on that occasion, aware of the dangers involved, that he uttered one of his more memorable remarks: 'Gentlemen, we must indeed all hang together, or, most assuredly, we shall all hang separately.'

But even when embroiled in politics before and after Independence, Franklin had time for scientific matters. It was he, for example, living in Paris in 1780 as US Ambassador to France, who first suggested 'Daylight Saving Time' as a device for increasing the number of useful hours in the working day. He explained his novel idea in great detail to the Parisians, but they seem to have taken little notice; no doubt with their own Revolution on the way, they had more important things to think about.

THE PATHFINDER OF
THE SEAS

24 January 2006 ∿

A wedding took place in Dublin in 1716, which had profound implications for the future of international meteorology. Mary Anne was the 26-year-old daughter of James Fontaine, a Huguenot who had been obliged to flee from France in 1685 following the revocation by Louis xiv of the Edict of Nantes. The groom was Matthew Maury, also a Frenchman, who had moved to Ireland from Gascony two years previously. The pair emigrated to Virginia in 1718, and were the great-grandparents of Matthew Fontaine Maury, one of the most illustrious names in the history of oceanography and meteorology.

Matthew was born 200 years ago today, on 24 January 1806, and grew up in Virginia and Tennessee. He joined the Navy at 19 and seemed set for a distinguished sea-faring career, but a stage-coach accident in 1839 ended this ambition. Unfit for active service, he was given what might have been a sinecure as Superintendent of the Naval Hydrographic Office.

But Lt Maury was a man of energy. One of the first tasks he set himself in his new post was to exploit the vast amount of hydro-logical and meteorological information available from the log books of naval and merchant vessels. To supplement these data, he furnished blank charts to sea captains, encouraging them to make daily records of weather and ocean conditions. In 1851 he began to publish his findings. He produced a comprehensive series of charts which mapped the currents and prevailing winds of the world's oceans in much greater detail than had ever been available before; they revolutionised navigational techniques, and within a year or two it was estimated that Maury was saving international commerce $50 million a year by dramatically reducing the duration of long-distance ocean voyages.

Another of his ventures concerned the mapping of the seabed, particularly that of the North Atlantic, which became a matter of very practical interest when it was decided to lay a cable from the US to Europe. Maury compiled all the information available from depth soundings; by 1850 he had produced a contour map of the bottom of the entire Atlantic, although it was to be another fifteen years, punctuated by many breaks and failures, before a trans-Atlantic cable finally came into operation.

These activities made Maury famous even in his own lifetime, and gave him his soubriquet 'the pathfinder of the seas'. But meteorologists remember him for quite a different reason: virtually single-handed, he organised the First International Meteorological Conference in Brussels in 1853, from which the development of the World Meteorological Organization can be traced.

Maury's later years were not without vicissitude. He lost what money he had in the American Civil War of the 1860s, and spent some time in very poor circumstances. In 1868, however, he was appointed professor of meteorology at the Virginia Military Institute, a post he held until his death at Lexington in February 1873.

THE ART OF THE POSSIBLE

25 *January* 2006 ～

I f the land of Ireland were entirely flat and leak-proof, and if its surface were bone-dry on 1 January and none of the rain that fell during the twelve succeeding months were allowed to escape or to evaporate, then by the end of December in a typical year the country would be inundated to a depth of slightly over one metre.

That, in theory, is what the rainfall figures tell us. Of course it is all nonsense, because, apart from other considerations, if our island were entirely flat and leak-proof, our national rainfall pattern would be changed unrecognisably, and so the depth of water would be something else entirely. In any event, we are able to make spurious assertions like the one above by virtue of the fact that we carefully measure rainfall at hundreds of places around the country.

The instrument we use to do so has changed little since the very earliest times. Those deployed nowadays have a funnel five inches in diameter to catch the water; the catch drains into a bottle, which is now assumed to contain the amount of rain which has fallen on the 5-inch circle above. Elementary mathematics then yields a figure in millimetres or inches, as required, which it is hoped will approximate to 'the depth to which a flat and impermeable surface would be covered by water in a given period, assuming that none of the liquid disappears by run-off or evaporation'.

Several factors, however, diminish the accuracy of measurement. Some of the rain adheres to the sides of the funnel and may evaporate without entering the bottle. Then, if the rain is heavy, some of it is lost by splashing out of the funnel, or rain which falls on the ground nearby may splash in. And by far the greatest error arises from the wind; the rain-gauge itself, projecting above the ground, causes swirls and eddies in the local airflow which result in a loss of catch. This could be avoided, of course, by sinking the instrument into the soil with the top of the funnel flush with the ground, but then the 'splashing' problem becomes noticeably worse.

To minimise these undesirable effects, the site for a rain-gauge is chosen very carefully. The instrument is also installed with great precision, making sure that it is exactly level and that the funnel is the correct, standard height above the ground. Even with the very best precautions, a gauge will often underestimate the rainfall by as much as 5 to 10 per cent, and in addition, when compiling rainfall figures the contents of the gauge must be assumed to be representative of the rainfall pattern over an area of several square miles in its vicinity—which it may not be. But as Bismarck said, *Die Politik ist die Lehre von Moeglichen*: 'Politics is the art of the possible,' and so it is, too, with meteorology.

METEOROLOGICAL APATHY AND AMADEUS

27 January 2006 ∾

You may not have heard, but today is Mozart's birthday. He was born in Salzburg on 27 January 1756, and while he was, one must admit, an excellent musician, he is meteorologically very disappointing.

Europe in Mozart's day was emerging from the rigours of the Little Ice Age, and although the average temperature of the region was increasing, the climate was erratic; it was an age of extremes, with harsh winters often alternating with hot, dry summers which brought drought and famine. Perhaps it was this very volatility which gave the weather its fascination for Viennese composers. In any event, most were adept at its portrayal through their music, and used the transition from one type of weather to another to enhance the dramatic impact of their renderings.

Three near contemporaries of Mozart stand out in this respect. Perhaps the best known 'weather-work' is *The Four Seasons*, written in 1725 by Antonio Vivaldi who, although Italian by birth, spent much of his life in Vienna. In 'Spring', for example, although the overall theme is one of joy and relief at the receding grip of a hard winter, the changeable nature of the season is illustrated by the inclusion of a brief thundershower. Later a more violent and lengthy thunderstorm breaks out to disrupt temporarily the hot, humid adagio of high 'Summer'; later passages suggest the shivers of wintertime, before the final allegro portrays fun and games on ice in a chilly, boisterous wind.

Franz Joseph Haydn, a good friend of Mozart's, also wrote about *The Seasons*. His oratorio of that name describes musically the brash renaissance of the earth from winter, the hot and sultry breezes of midsummer, and the hunting festivals of autumn. But he could also compose to a much shorter timescale; around 1761 he produced three short symphonies called *Le Matin*, *Le Midi*, and *Le Soir*—what one might describe as a 'diurnal suite'. The opening of the first portrays the dawn, while the second is suggestive of the harsh bright sunshine of midday; the third symphony concludes with a vigorous movement unambiguously labelled 'La Tempesta'. Although Haydn placed his thundershower in the late evening, meteorological savants might quibble that the thunderstorm frequency in most parts of central Europe peaks in the late afternoon.

And Haydn's pupil, Beethoven, who came to Vienna very shortly after Mozart's death, also had a rural bent. His Sixth

Symphony, the *Pastoral*, describes in vivid detail the progression of a brief but violent thunderstorm which dominates the local landscape.

But Mozart? Wolfgang Amadeus, sadly, appears to have had little interest in the weather. Unlike his fellow composers, he made few attempts throughout his 700 compositions to play the weather in any major key. Even he, however, was not totally resistant to meteorological temptation: terrifying thunder can be heard in *Don Giovanni*, and Contradance K.534, *The Thunderstorm*, also fulfils all the lively promise of its name.

WHEN HAS SPRING SPRUNG?

2 February 2006 ∽

In these temperate latitudes, spring is seen as a time of hope and fresh beginnings, when the world awakes from the deep sleep of winter and new life surges from the earth; it is a season of procreation and of new vitality. Even the name itself, which in old English was restricted in meaning to either the source of a stream or the act of leaping, has connotations of newness and unaccustomed energy. But only in the fifteenth century did the word 'springtime' evolve to mean a time when the world, as it were, leaps to its feet, and new life springs from the ground. Later, textual references to, for example, 'the spring of the leaf' were shortened to just merely 'spring', by which time, etymologically at least, it could be said the season had arrived.

But when does it arrive in real life? The start of spring is a subjective concept; it begins more or less whenever you want it to begin. In parts of Ireland and Britain, the popular view is that spring begins on 1 February, St Bridget's Day. To many, however, this date is spuriously early, and gardeners, meteorologists and astronomers all agree to differ on the question, each group having its own criteria—and all with very good reason in the context of their spheres of interest.

One way of deciding when the season has arrived is to watch for the budding of the local plant life. According to the old proverb, it is not spring until you can plant your foot upon twelve daisies, but modern technology allows us to watch more systematically the progress of the seasons. Around this time of year or a little later, a 'green wave' can be observed on successive satellite images moving northwards at an average rate of about 100 miles a week. Interestingly, it has been discovered that since satellite observations began some 40 years ago, the onset of spring in the northern hemisphere has been getting earlier each year, occurring on average about ten days sooner now than it did in the middle of the 1960s. And this, of course, is entirely consistent with current theories about global warming.

Astronomers have another angle. To them, winter is the period from the winter solstice—around 21 December, when the Sun is at its most southerly point over the Tropic of Capricorn—until the vernal equinox, when the Sun crosses the equator again on its seasonal passage northwards. Astronomical spring, then, begins on 21 March, or thereabouts.

But weatherpeople have their own ideas—and with an understandable chauvinism, they believe it to be the most logical; they base it on the weather. Meteorologists regard the winter months as being the three coldest ones of the year on average: December, January and February. So for them, the season of spring does not begin for another month, until 1 March.

THE TRUE STORY OF SODOM AND GOMORRAH

3 February 2006 ∿

There are few natural disasters, if any, that do not merit a verse, or even a chapter, in the Bible. The ten plagues of Egypt, for example, run the gamut of human misery, neatly packaged all in one portfolio; and then we have Noah's flood, the collapsing walls of Jericho, and the destruction of Sodom and Gomorrah. Many of these episodes are cleverly disguised as miracles, and as in the case of the theological and moral principles the Holy Book contains, it takes skilled analysis by a suitably inspired interpreter before an *ex cathedra* pronouncement can be made identifying any given phenomenon for what it really is.

Take, for example, the queer happenings at Sodom and Gomorrah. God in heaven was thoroughly disgusted by the goings on in these two cities, and dropped a hint to Abraham that he was going to 'take them out'. Abraham, however, bargained with him: 'If there be fifty just men in the city, shall they perish too?' he asked the Lord. 'Will you not spare the place for the sake of the fifty just?' The Lord agreed, but Abraham could not find fifty just men. After much pleading with the Almighty, it was decided that if he could find forty-five, then later forty, the cities would be spared. Abraham persisted down to ten, whereupon God declared this to be his final offer. But of course, not ten, but only *one* just man was found—and he was Lot.

The Lord compromised, however, by sending two angels down to Sodom to suggest to Lot that he evacuate. And comely lads they must have been, because no sooner had they settled down in *chez* Lot, than the entire male citizenry of Sodom gathered at the door, and only by supernatural subterfuge was a very nasty incident avoided. In any event, the following day the angels escorted Lot and his family from the city, and as down the road they went 'The Lord rained upon Sodom and Gomorrah brimstone and fire from out of heaven. And he destroyed those cities and the country round about.'

So much for the facts. But scientists like to suggest ways by which the Almighty might have achieved his desired objective, and in the case of Sodom and Gomorrah, it seems, the key may well be earthquakes.

Although no one knows exactly where they were, the two cities are assumed to have been near the Dead Sea, or perhaps even underneath it as we know it now. There is a well-known geological fault in the vicinity, and the theory is that a tremor may first have partially destroyed the towns, while at the same time the friction of the sliding plates generated sufficient heat to ignite subterranean oil and bitumen deposits. The blaze, which finished off both Sodom and Gomorrah, would have been so fierce that the whole region would have seemed to be on fire—as if, in fact, it had indeed been rained upon by fire and brimstone.

HIGH PRESSURE WINTER GLOOM

6 February 2006 ∾

Anticyclones, as we have seen of late here in the vicinity of Ireland, meander slowly around the weather chart with none of the militant sense of purpose of your typical depression. In fact, one could almost say that anticyclones exist merely because there are no depressions in the vicinity at the time. When accompanied by clear skies, winter anticyclones allow the Earth to lose heat very rapidly at night, so that while the following morning may be bright and sunny, the ground is often hard with frost. Just as easily, however, as has happened recently, anticyclones are dull and listless features of the winter weather catalogue, whose overcast skies are parsimonious with sunshine, producing the phenomenon we know as *anticyclonic gloom*.

Both lows and highs are three-dimensional phenomena. The air around a depression spirals inwards towards the centre where it is then forced to ascend in vigorous updrafts, but anticyclones, by contrast, are regions of gentle but widespread descent of air, a phenomenon we know as *subsidence*. The descending air is subject to compression, which causes it to become warmer than it previously was, and the consequent drop in the relative humidity sometimes ensures that there is very little cloud.

But subsidence occurs only down to within a thousand feet or so of the ground. The warm, dry air above this level, superimposed on colder air near the surface, often results in winter in what we call a 'temperature inversion'; in effect, the warm air aloft acts as a lid on the lower atmosphere and cuts off any tendency for it to bubble upwards in vertical currents of rising air. Natural ventilation near ground level is further reduced by the light winds or calms typically prevailing near the centre of an anticyclone. Into this imprisoned air adjacent to the Earth's surface go the smoke and other pollutants from domestic and industrial chimneys and from the exhaust-pipes of motor vehicles, and as their concentrations build up over the days, visibility is reduced, producing haze or even smog.

Moreover, if the humidity a short distance above the ground is high enough for cloud to form, this cloud is obliged to spread horizontally in a thick uniform sheet just below the discontinuity of temperature; this, combined with the weak winter sunshine, produces the condition prevalent in recent days known to meteorologists as anticyclonic gloom.

It is no consolation to those confined under this murky blanket that the layer affected is very shallow. Above the inversion the warm, dry, subsided air of the anticyclone is crystal clear. Aeroplanes ascending from an airport shrouded in anticyclonic gloom reach clear air almost immediately, and indeed an observer on the summit of a nearby hill in such conditions may sometimes find himself in sunlight, looking down on a carpet of cloud and haze below.

A DIVINE GIFT WITH A DOWNSIDE

7 February 2006 ～

It was Prometheus—or so the story goes—who first presented us with fire. Unknown to Zeus, the chief god of the ancient Greeks, he lit a torch at the golden chariot of the Sun, and sneaking it out of heaven by a subterfuge, he conferred on humankind a singular advantage over other creatures. Meteorologists, of course, suspect that it was not Prometheus, but lightning, that began it all; either way, the gift has great destructive power when unconstrained and this has been the case in parts of County Kerry in the last few days.

Every year, more than 1,000 acres of Irish trees are totally destroyed by fire. There are few fires from September to January, but the incidence rises rapidly from February until around late

April and early May, and then falls off markedly by June. This, very clearly, is because the flammability of the environment varies with the seasons, being lowest in autumn and winter when it is saturated with moisture, and low also in midsummer when there is a fresh flush of green growth; it is high in spring when the vegetation is often dried up by cold easterly winds, and sometimes also in late summer if it has been scorched by the Sun and dried by drought. It is no coincidence, moreover, that April and May are the peak months, because these, on average, are the two driest months of the year in most parts of Ireland; neither is it any coincidence that gorse fires have become a problem earlier than usual this year, since rainfall totals so far have been running at less than 50 per cent of normal values.

The specific causes of about 70 per cent of bush or forest fires remain unknown, while data for the other 30 per cent suggest that most have their origins in human activities of some kind, usually a consequence of carelessness. Some, for example, are the accidental result of activities related to forestry itself, or undertaken in the course of agriculture, and a few now and then are clearly deliberate and malevolent in intent. Lightning is a common source of ignition, although it cannot be blamed for the recent outbreaks, and neither at this time of year, and particularly in the cloudy conditions experienced of late, can another common cause: bright sunshine focused to a point by broken glass, providing a tiny but effective solar furnace.

Once a dry spell has extracted the moisture from the vegetation, then, whatever the spark, 'a little fire', as Shakespeare puts it, 'is quickly trodden out, which being suffer'd rivers cannot quench.' Each active fire area provides the heat necessary to raise the temperature of adjacent fuel to ignition temperature, and any wind that may be present facilitates this transfer by deflecting flames and heated columns of air away from the vertical, bringing them into contact with adjacent vegetation.

| DEADLY FALLS OF SNOW

8 *February* 2006 ~

S tatistically speaking, an avalanche is a pretty harmless thing. Compared to other natural hazards, they cause relatively few fatalities and do little harm to property, ranking well below volcanoes in these respects and somewhere on a par with land-slides. But these small losses do not stem from any scarcity of avalanches around the world; the reason is that the vast majority occur in uninhabited areas, and for every one that hits the news, a thousand others cascade down their own secluded mountains, *incognito*. Perhaps it is the sheer unluckiness of the victims which underlines their tragedy.

Most avalanches happen on slopes with a gradient of between 30 and 45 degrees. As a general rule the 'north wind's masonry' first arranges the 'frolic architecture of the snow' in such a way as to bring about a structure which is unstable; all it needs then is some mechanical or meteorological trigger to send thousands of tons of snow cascading down the mountainside at staggering speeds. Dry snow can move at up to 200 mph; wet snow travels more slowly, but causes greater damage because of its increased weight.

An avalanche is liable to occur when a slab of strong, cohesive snow rests on top of a layer that is much more soft and crumbly. The former is composed of crystals that are 'spiky', so that the individual flakes become locked together; smooth crystals without any jagged edges, on the other hand, produce weak 'sugar snow' from which the surface layer may shear away to start the avalanche.

If conditions are right, an avalanche can be triggered by a loud noise. Indeed, in some countries explosions are detonated in order to start avalanches in controlled conditions—to get them over with, as it were. But even the passage of a single skier across the surface of the snow may sometimes be enough to provide the necessary stimulus.

Meteorological factors are also important. An increase in temperature often causes a weakening of the bonds between the individual ice granules; if the temperature rise continues, it may result in a thin film of water around each granule, which acts as a lubricator and facilitates movement. This effect is greatest with an approaching thaw, so springtime—from now on, indeed—is often the most dangerous time of year. And for the same reason, ava- lanches often occur most readily on slopes which catch the Sun.

Rain or snow may also be a trigger. Rain percolates into the snow beneath the surface, and weakens the bonds between the different layers. And both rain and extra snow increase the shearing force, by adding weight to an accumulation near the top; this is particularly dangerous on shallow slopes, because a large amount of fresh snow can be accommodated before the critical shearing force is reached—but then the amount of snow released is very great.

NEPTUNE IN AN APATHETIC MOOD

9 February 2006 ∿

The weather has been ominously calm of late. This is indeed unusual, since a vigorous storm or two in January and February is very much more the norm than the exception. And as it happens, this date, the 9th, has been a favourite for February storms.

A very intense event ten years ago today, on 9 February 1996, caused widespread damage throughout the country. Then eight years previously, on 9 February 1988, an even more violent storm passed to the northwest of Ireland, close to Donegal, and caused severe damage to property and several deaths. And another reminder of severe weather on this date can be found on the East Pier at Dún Laoghaire where a memorial recalls the fate of the *Neptune* 145 years ago today, on 9 February 1861.

Neptune, as we know, was the Roman god of the sea. He would surge across the waves in his golden chariot, surrounded by dolphins and other creatures of the deep, and wielding a trident, the symbol of his power. He was capable of summoning terrible storms, and taking the lives of those he thought were disrespectful, but he could also calm the waters if he wanted to.

He did just that, for example, during the voyage of Aeneas and his fellow Trojans following the siege of Troy. The emigrating warriors were making good progress along the Mediterranean, heading for the spot that one day would be Rome, when they were seen by Juno. This wife of Jupiter had a score to settle, and saw her opportunity. She hurried to Aeolus, he to whom Jupiter had entrusted government of the winds, and instructed him to organise a storm. Anxious, no doubt, not to offend the boss's wife, Aeolus complied with her wishes, and the Trojan ships were stranded on the rocks.

Neptune, however, seems to have resented this intrusion in his bailiwick. In any event, he dismissed the winds immediately, brushed the clouds from the face of the Sun, and personally prised the Trojan ships from the rocks with his own trident. Thus, to quote the poet Edmund Waller:

> *Above the waves did Neptune show his face,*
> *To chide the winds and save the Trojan race.*

This god of the sea, however, was less obliging in Irish waters on
this day in 1861, and did nothing to quell the violent storm in
Dublin Bay which wrecked the sailing ship named after him. The
memorial on the East Pier commemorates Captain J. McNeill
Boyd and five men from another ship, the *Ajax*, who perished in
their gallant efforts to save the *Neptune*'s crew. And it features in
Samuel Beckett's storm from *Krapp's Last Tape*:

> . . . *great granite rocks the foam flying up in the light
> of the lighthouse and the wind-gauge spinning like a
> propeller clear to me at last . . . .*

THE ANCIENT WAVES OF IRELAND

11 *February* 2006 ∽

A round the time, long, long ago, when the children of Lir
were living out their endless years as swans and Finn
McCool and the Fianna righted wrongs throughout the
length and breadth of Ireland, a series of powerful ocean waves
approached our coasts. These, as far as we know, were not
tsunami, nor even 'freak waves' in the sense in which we understand the terms today. They were magic waves of such power that
when the chronicler of the adventures of Deirdre and the sons of
Usnach sought a metaphor for the ferocity of the clash between
Fiacre and Iollan the Fair, he described it as if 'the three great
waves of Éire, the bank-overflowing, white-foaming, curled wave

of Cliodhna, the long-sided steady wave of Tuagh, and the great right-courageous wave of Rudhraighe, had all arisen together to smother one another'.

Cliodhna's wave is said to have occurred at Glandore in County Cork. Cliodhna of the Fair Hair, one of the mystical Tuatha De Danann, was the beautiful daughter of Gebann, a chief druid of Tír na nÓg, the country of the sea god, Manannan Mac Lir. Cliodhna fell madly in love with Caoimhin of the Curling Locks, a dissident member of the Fianna who had been expelled for immorality, and who at this stage in his wanderings had ended up in Tír na nÓg.

The pair eloped together in a curragh, landing eventually at Glandore where Caoimhin went ashore to hunt for deer, leaving Cliodhna in the boat. 'But the people of Manannan's house came after them, having forty ships. And Iuchnu, that was in the cur-ragh with Cliodhna, did treachery, and he played music to her till she lay down in the boat and fell asleep. And then a great wave came up on the strand and swept her away and delivered her back to her fairy kingdom.'

Manannan was also involved in the great wave of Tuagh, although on this occasion the elements seem to have worked against him. The story goes that Conall Collomrach, high king of Ireland at the time, had a beautiful daughter called Tuagh. Manannan lusted after Tuagh, and sent one of his men, Fir Fi Mac Evgabail, to kidnap her, which he did by casting a spell to put her into a deep sleep. He brought her to the mouth of the river Bann and left her there asleep while he went to fetch a boat to bring her out to sea to Manannan. But while she slept, a huge wave came in and carried her off, and the beautiful Tuagh was drowned. In her memory, we are told, the mouth of the Bann was renamed *Tuaigh Inbhir*.

The wave of Rudhraighe, which occurred in Dundrum Bay in County Down, has similar roots in Celtic mythology, as indeed does a fourth wave which inundated the countryside around Ballyshannon, County Donegal—the wave of Assaroe. But these are other stories.

A FATAL FROST FOR BUILDING BESS

13 *February* 2006 ∾

T he winters were severe in England in the first decade of the seventeenth century, and coldest of all was that of 1607/08, when a severe frost lasted continuously from 5 December until well into February. In London the Thames froze solid, with fires being lit upon the ice, and around the country, water mills seized up with frozen streams and rivers. Farther north, in Derbyshire, the hard frost is said to have fulfilled a prophesy concerning Bess of Hardwicke.

Elizabeth Hardwicke was born in 1527 into a moderately prosperous, land-owning family of Derbyshire. At the age of 14, Bess was married to one Richard Barlow, but young Richard, no older than his bride, died before the marriage could be consummated. Later Elizabeth married Sir William Cavendish, and having survived this Sir William, married yet another, Sir William St Loe. On the latter's death she married, finally, George Talbot, sixth earl of Shrewsbury.

Bess is chiefly remembered on two grounds. Firstly, in 1569 her husband, Shrewsbury, was appointed by Queen Elizabeth I to be custodian-gaoler of Mary, Queen of Scots. Bess was much in contact with the captive queen, and made of her something of a confidante; she repeated to Mary all the gossip of the time, much of it graphically suggesting that the Virgin Queen, Elizabeth, was undeserving of the sobriquet. Elizabeth in due course came to hear of this, and Bess of Hardwicke had much explaining to do before the Queen and Council. But Bess, resourceful woman that she was, survived.

Bess's other claim to fame explains why she was known in her time as 'Building Bess of Hardwicke'. She was a shrewd business-woman, and accumulated great wealth over the years as each of her four husbands died in turn, to the extent that in her later years she was accounted the wealthiest woman in England next to Queen Elizabeth. She was particularly fond of renovating and extending all her various properties, and of adding from time to time to her portfolio.

It is said of Bess that, as she advanced in years, a fortune-teller told her that she need have no fear of dying as long as she con-tinued building. So Bess continued, completing a succession of magnificent mansions, including Hardwicke Hall, Bolsover, Oldcotes, Worksop and Chatsworth. But then came the winter of 1607/08. It was cold and harsh, with a long, uninterrupted frost, and the builders' labourers were no longer able to continue with their work. They tried to mix the mortar with hot ale, but the cold was too severe. And as foretold, before any building could resume, Bess of Hardwicke died 398 years ago today, on 13 February 1608.

Climatological history, however, shows Bess to have been most unlucky. A thaw came just 24 hours after she had died; spring arrived on 14 February 1608, temperatures rose, and the frost that did for Bess of Hardwicke disappeared.

A BLIZZARD VINDICATED

15 February 2006 ◠

The weekend blizzards in New York and its environs broke many records in terms of accumulated snowfall. They were reminiscent of one of the most devastating events in American weather history, the famous 'Great Blizzard of '88' which buried the eastern seaboard from Maryland to Maine under four or five feet of snow, causing many deaths, in March 1888. For three days, from the 12th to the 14th of that month, storm-force winds, heavy snow and temperatures several degrees below zero brought life in the affected areas to a standstill.

The 1888 storm also has the distinction of being the phenomenon that brought the word 'blizzard' into widespread use. The term first appeared, apparently, in 1870 in *The Northern Vindicator*, a local newspaper in the Iowa town of Esterville. Many of the early settlers in Iowa came from Germany, and when they experienced the severe winter storms on the Great Plains, they would exclaim, according to the *Vindicator*, '*Der Sturm kommt blitzartig*': 'The storm comes like lightning.' The transition from blitzartig to 'blizzard', the paper said, was a natural, even if not entirely logical, progression in linguistics. But no one outside Iowa had heard of 'blizzards' until the term was widely applied in the national newspapers to the blizzard of '88.

Interestingly, the depression which caused the 1888 storm made its way across the Atlantic in the succeeding days, along a track that appears to be rather similar to that being followed by last weekend's New York storm. This latter is expected to be located off the coast of Donegal tomorrow, and seems set to bring us gales and strong winds. Blizzards, at the time of writing, are definitely not expected, but this was not the case in 1888; on that occasion the storm hit Britain on 18 March, and brought with it a significant amount of snow, in addition to the strong winds. Understandably, newspapers on this side of the Atlantic continued to refer to it as the 'blizzard'.

But they worried about the etymology of the word. Having dismissed as frivolous an explanation that such a storm might be named after a Blizzard family of Buckinghamshire who had emigrated to America some years previously, *The Times* pronounced the source to be an expression of the English midlands: 'Well, I be blizzered,' apparently, was a common pronouncement by persons amazed by an item of very startling news.

'Nonsense!' replied *The New York Times* from across the water, and ignoring the Germans down in Iowa, it declared: 'It is merely a bit of onomatopoeia. Like the hoof-beats in Virgil's poetry, the word is simply supposed to sound, more or less, like the thing that it denotes.'

By 19 March the now famous blizzard had moved across the English Channel to the Continent, and the German newspapers had to have their pfennig-worth. Naturally they favoured Iowa, and proclaimed that the word was definitely German after all.

MACH WAS SOMETHING OF A POLYMATH

18 *February* 2006 ∿

Ernst Mach was born in what is now the Czech Republic in 1838. He qualified in mathematics, physics and philosophy and held professorships in all three disciplines at various stages in his long career. He died 90 years ago tomorrow, on 19 February 1916.

Now, Mach was something of a polymath. In 1877 he correctly deduced by mathematics the sound effects likely to be produced by a projectile travelling faster than the speed of sound, essentially predicting the occurrence of the now familiar sonic boom. For this achievement he was given the posthumous honour of being the eponym for the method by which we measure supersonic speed.

His ideas on the philosophy of science were also greatly influential in the development of the twentieth-century concept of *logical positivism*, and to the perception of philosophy as analytical, rather than speculative, inquiry. But less well known, perhaps, is Mach's contribution to meteorological optics. He identified as an optical illusion the appearance, in certain circumstances, of two anomalous bands of light, one bright and one dark, which have come to be known as *Mach bands*.

The phenomenon is best illustrated by imagining a sheet of cardboard casting a dark shadow on a white surface in bright sunlight. Between the shadow and the illuminated part of the surface is a 'half-shadow', a consequence of the finite dimensions of the solar disc; parts of the surface near the edge of the shadow are illuminated by, perhaps, half the solar disc, so that the transition from light to shadow is gradual rather than sharply defined. But if you look very closely, you will see that the half-shadow has an extra-bright edge on the illuminated side and an extra-dark band near the dark boundary of the half-shadow. These are the two Mach bands.

Instruments sensitive to light reveal that these bands have no real existence. Their perception by a human observer is thought to be due to small movements of the eye, or to the weakened sensitivity of the retina in the neighbourhood of its illuminated parts.

In everyday life, the phenomenon is apparent when looking at a building which temporarily masks the Sun; the outline of the building appears to be edged with light. And a similar effect can be seen even more clearly when viewing from an elevated site a succession of ridges in a gently undulating countryside. It is common experience that successive ridges become lighter and lighter because of the atmospheric attenuation of their reflected light, and that they finally become lost to sight in the hazy distance. But look more closely, and you will notice that each ridge looks darker along its top than along its base. This, however, is an illusion, arising from the fact that each ridge is bounded along its top by a lighter strip, and along its base by a darker strip. Try it sometime, and see!

SPYING ON THE WEATHER

20 *February* 2006 ∿

A subtle distinction that young meteorologists of my generation were required to grasp was the difference between a cipher and a code. The former, we were told, was used by spies to exchange secret information in a form that no one else could understand. A message in code, on the other hand, although at first glance as indecipherable as any cipher, was intended to be read by anyone who wished to do so, and its key, as a general rule, was readily to hand. Typical of the latter, it was said, were the METAR and TAF codes, as used by meteorologists.

Before departure, a pilot naturally wishes to know the kind of weather to expect when landing at the destination. He or she will therefore first look at a METAR for the relevant airport. METAR stands for 'Meteorological Report', and gives in coded form a summary of the weather at a particular aerodrome for a particular time. For example, a pilot at Shannon contemplating taking off for Liverpool would have access to the following message:

METAR EGGP 201300Z 04005 KT 9000 SHRA SCT018 03/02 Q1007

Here EGGP is the identifying indicator for Liverpool Airport, and 201300 tells the pilot that what follows describes the weather at 1300 GMT on the 20th of the month. The whole message, therefore, reads: 'At 1pm Liverpool was experiencing a light breeze of five knots, blowing from the northeast or 040 degrees; the visibility was 9 kilometres in a shower of rain, with a broken layer of cloud 1,800 feet above the ground; the temperature was three degrees Celsius, the dew point (a measure of humidity) two degrees, and the correct pressure altimeter setting for an aircraft about to land at Liverpool would be 1007 hectopascals.'

This, of course, only tells the pilot what the weather looks like *now*, and not what it will be like when the aeroplane arrives. For this he or she will need a TAF, a Terminal Aerodrome Forecast, which gives, in similar code, a summary of expected conditions over the next nine hours or so. The TAF might look like:

TAF EGGP 201322 VRB07KT 9999 BKN025 TEMPO 1316 3000 SHRASN BKN005

Roughly translated, it reads: 'During the period from 1300 to 2200 on the 20th, the wind of around seven knots will be variable in direction, the visibility generally will be greater than 10 km, and there will be broken cloud around 2,500 feet above the ground; temporarily, however, now and then between 1300 and 1600, showers of rain or snow will reduce the visibility to 3 km, and the cloud base will descend to around 500 feet.'

Knowing the conditions to be well within the aircraft's capabilities, the captain can confidently issue the order to switch the doors from manual and have them armed and cross-checked—although what that may mean is quite another story.

THE MANY GUISES OF DERWENTWATER'S LIGHTS

24 February 2006 ∿

James Radcliffe, third earl of Derwentwater, was a staunch supporter of the Old Pretender to the English throne—he who, you may remember, was ex-King James II's son and father of the Young Pretender, Charlie, fondly known as 'Bonnie'. The earl played a prominent part in the 1715 Rebellion in the Stuart cause, and was subsequently captured and sentenced to death for treason. He was beheaded on Tower Hill in London 290 years ago today, on 24 February 1716.

One of the laird's legacies to posterity was 'Derwentwater's Farewell', allegedly written by him on the night before he died:

> *Farewell each friendly, well-known face,*
> *My heart has held so dear,*
> *My tenants now must leave their lands*
> *Or hold their lives in fear.*
> *Then fare thee well, brave Witherington,*
> *Since fate has put us down,*
> *If thou and I have lost our lives*
> *Our King has lost his crown.*

And so it goes for many maudlin verses. But another feature of the night before Lord Derwentwater's death, it is said, was an exceptionally brilliant display of the aurora, and so the phenomenon, in Scottish eyes, became associated with the earl's untimely fate as 'Lord Derwentwater's lights'.

Others gave them different names. In classical times they called them *candissimi fumi*, 'streams of the most brilliant kind'; the Norsemen of old thought of them as *Vindlys*, 'the wind-lights', because, when brighter than usual, they were seen as heralding the first great storm of winter; sometimes the French would refer to them as 'the dancing goats', *les chevres dansantes*; and here in Ireland came *na saighneáin*, 'the spears of light'.

The aurorae borealis have been a common feature of the northern skies since time began, and at their best they are a brilliant spectacle of restlessly moving, coloured streamers, conveying an eerie aura of unearthly splendour. In the auroral zone of maximum frequency, a region which extends from the north of Norway, south of Iceland and Greenland, over northern Canada to the north of Siberia, the phenomenon can be seen almost every night the sky is clear. In these latitudes, the northern lights are seen on about 5 per cent of occasions when conditions otherwise are suitable, appearing low in the sky near the northern horizon as a kind of grey-white glow with a sharp lower border.

On rare occasions the aurorae are in evidence even farther

from the pole. The historian Flavius Josephus, for example, tells us that the Jewish revolt against the Romans in AD67 was preceded by fiery chariots and armed battalions racing across the northern sky. Modern revisionists, however, have concluded that this flamboyant portent of rebellion was probably Lord Derwentwater's lights in yet another guise; they are very unusual as far south as Jerusalem, but not unknown.

| WAITING FOR THE CHINOOK

25 *February* 2006 ∽

The story goes that in the early spring of 1886, a young American artist, Charles M. Russell, was eking out a living as an unknown range rider in Montana. His employers 'back east', it seems, were worried about the effects of the harsh winter on their livestock, and asked for a report. Instead of using pen and ink, Russell took up his brush, and sent them a painting— a work that has become a powerful symbol, iconic of the hardships endured in the heyday of the old-time western ranching.

The painting shows the vast inhospitable Great Plains thick with snow, and a few starving coyotes, too weak to kill, circling hungrily around the last surviving steer, waiting for it to die from cold. The painting, now a very famous work, is called 'Waiting for the Chinook'.

The chinook is a warm, dry wind that sweeps down the eastern side of the Rocky Mountains in the early spring. It takes its name from the fact that it blew from 'over the Chinook camp' to the trading post established by the Hudson Bay Company at Astoria in the territory of Oregon; and even today, its sudden onset is eagerly awaited by the inhabitants of that State, and of Wyoming, Colorado and Montana.

Air, as we know, cools if it is allowed to expand, and increases in temperature if it is compressed. But the unusual warmth of the chinook arises from the fact that the temperature of *dry* air changes much more rapidly in this way than is the case with *moist* air.

A moist, westerly flow of air approaching the US from the Pacific is forced to ascend over the Rockies in its path. As it moves upwards, the air expands and cools, and in due course its temperature falls sufficiently for condensation to take place; much of its moisture then falls to the ground as rain or snow. Consequently, as the wind passes over the crest of the mountains, it has already lost much of its moisture on the ascent; being now relatively dry, its temperature rises very quickly with compression as it descends, and by the time the air reaches the plains, it may be 10 or 15 degrees warmer than it was before it began to cross the mountain barrier. This is the chinook.

A chinook which suddenly displaces a pool of cold, winter air that has been stagnant for weeks over the Great Plains often results in local temperature increases of as much as 20°C in less than half an hour. It is superbly efficient at clearing away, in the space of a few hours, the blanket of snow remaining after the long, harsh North American winter, and is therefore sometimes called the 'snow-eater'. And, clearly, the characteristics of this warm wind lie behind the title of Russell's famous painting; the lone steer's only hope of survival is a timely onset of the benevolent chinook.

AN ALTERNATIVE
CHRONICLER OF HIS TIMES

27 *February* 2006 〜

Everybody knows of Samuel Pepys and of his Diary written in the 1660s. But Pepys's mildly picaresque adventures unfairly overshadow the more sober scribblings of another diarist of the same period. John Evelyn recorded his *Memoirs*, day by day in meticulous detail, for more than half a century, as opposed to the mere nine years and five months covered by the narrative entries of Samuel Pepys.

Evelyn was born in 1620, and was fortunate enough to be of independent wealth. For much of his long life he was what we nowadays would call a 'green activist', and was perhaps the first to protest publicly to the powers that be about the pollution of the London air. In 1661 he published *The Inconvenience of the Air and Smoke, or London Dissipated—Together with some Remedies Humbly Proposed*, better remembered by its Latin name of *Fumifugium*. In it he paints a graphic picture: 'The city of London resembles more the face of Mount Etna, the court of Vulcan, or Stromboli, or the suburbs of hell, than an assembly of rational creatures and the imperial seat of our incomparable monarch. For when in all other places the air is most serene and pure, it is here eclipsed with such clouds of sulphur that the Sun itself which gives day to all the world besides is hardly able to penetrate.'

Evelyn's diary, begun when he was eleven years old, is less spontaneous and personal than that of Samuel Pepys, but it gives a valuable insight into the English, and indeed the Continental, society of the time. He is one of our principal informants, for example, about the Great Fire of London in 1666. His entry for 3 September that year begins: 'This fatal night, at about ten o'clock, began that deplorable fire near Fish Street in London— a miserable and calamitous spectacle, such as happily the world had not seen the like since the foundation of it, nor would be out-done till the universal conflagration of it all.'

We also gain much insight from Evelyn's diaries into the severe harshness of the winters during the Little Ice Age, which was at its height around that time. In his entry for 24 January 1684, however, he describes nicely the compensatory pleasures of the freezing conditions: 'The Thames before London was still planted with booths in formal streets, and with all sorts of trades and shops furnished with commodities of all kinds. Coaches plied to and fro as if in the streets, and there was sliding, bull baiting, horse and coach races, puppet plays and other interludes, with tippling and other lewd entertainments—so that it all seemed to be a bacchanalian triumph, or a carnival upon the water.'

John Evelyn lived on for another 22 years, and died 300 years ago today, on 27 February 1706.

THE ARTISTRY OF FROST

3 *March* 2006 ∾

For quite some time in recent months I was under the impression that the RTÉ weather forecast on radio was spon-sored by a company called Jocul. I have since discovered that this is not the case, and that the sponsors are the manufacturers of a yoghurt called something else entirely, but for the duration of my misapprehension I was happy in the apparent appropriateness of an association with the little artist of the frost.

Some of us above a certain age will remember the 'ferns' of ice that used to form on the insides of our bedroom windowpanes on frosty winter mornings. It is a phenomenon unfamiliar to our children, because nowadays the temperature inside our double-glazed and heated homes is never low enough for it to happen. But the intricate patterns can still be seen from time to time on motor car windows in the aftermath of a clear and very frosty night.

The meteorological explanation is relatively simple. On a very cold night, the temperature of the inside surface of a single window-pane in an unheated room may fall well below the freezing point. Moreover, in the case of bedrooms, the moisture exuded through the night by the occupants increases the humidity of the air, often very close to saturation. The air rids itself of excess moisture by depositing it in the form of ice crystals, which form delicate patterns on the freezing glass. These window-crystals do not have the perfect symmetry of snow crystals formed in free air, but it is this very lack of symmetry that allows the patterns to take on such a great variety of magical, surreal shapes.

It used to be thought, however, that these icy logos were the handiwork of Jocul Frosti, a mythical elf-like creature in Scandinavian mythology. His name is a combination of Jocul, meaning 'icicle', and Frosti, meaning 'frost', and he had a strong artistic steak. His handiwork was to be seen when he turned the leaves of trees from green to brown each year with the approach of winter, and it was Jocul, too, who engraved the windowpanes with those elaborate patterns on nights when it was very, very cold.

Jocul Frosti came to be known as Jack Frost whenever he visited English-speaking countries, but there were parts of the world where he was never heard of. In Russia, for example, the icy artist was an old man called Father Frost, a blacksmith—or perhaps a 'whitesmith'—who would bind water and earth together with heavy silver chains. In Japan, the Frost Man was the slightly malevolent brother of the Mist Man; and in Germany, the author of the patterns was a woman, a cold, rather austere figure whom German children knew as Mother Frost, and who could cause it to snow simply by shaking out the white feathers from her bed.

A WIND THAT RECALLS THE ALAMO

6 *March* 2006 ∿

The eighteenth-century Franciscan missionary church in San Antonio, the *Alamo*, took its name from the Spanish word for the cottonwood trees indigenous to the locality. At the start of the struggle for independence from Mexico in December 1835, a small band of Texan volunteers occupied the Alamo, and on 23 February the following year they were surrounded by several thousand Mexican troops under General Antonio Lopez de Santa Anna. The insurgents held out until 6 March, but 170 years ago today the besiegers breached the outer wall, and Santa Anna having ordered that no prisoners should be taken, the 184 defenders, including Davy Crockett and Colonel Jim Bowie, were systematically slaughtered. Their feat of heroic resistance is remembered on 6 March each year as Alamo Day.

Antonio de Santa Anna was a complex individual. He possessed, it was said, a magnetic personality and real qualities of leadership, but he was also totally lacking in principle and became renowned for changing sides on nearly every major issue of the day. His subsequent activities led Mexico into a long series of disasters and visited ill-repute and tragedy upon the General himself.

Some said he had a wind named after him. The Santa Ana is a hot, dry, parching wind in southern California, laden with piercing particles of dust, which descends briskly through the Cajon and Santa Ana Passes to the Pacific coast. It is often referred to as a 'desert' wind—and indeed it is, since it originates in the Mojave Desert to the east of the Sierra Nevada mountains. Its warmth and dryness, however, come not from the desert, but from the process of compression; the plateau where the air originates is some 3,500 feet above sea level, and it is the increase in barometric pressure that this air experiences as it descends through the mountain valleys to the coast which endows the wind with its unpleasant characteristics.

In earlier days, when southern California was a sparsely populated agricultural region, the Santa Ana was mainly dreaded for the damage it did to orchards and to farmland. Today it is still feared for its destructive power, since it is sometimes strong enough to uproot trees and lift the roofs from houses, and also for the way it exacerbates California's periodic forest fires.

But any real connection with the Generalissimo has been discounted, if only because historical records have shown that neither he nor his famous dust-raising cavalry had ever been in southern California. It is now accepted that the name can be traced back to the discovery of the Santa Ana River valley by the Spaniard Gaspar de Portola, on St Anne's Day in 1769. Applied to the region's characteristic wind, however, the description was introduced into general use only in December 1901, by an Associated Press correspondent reporting from the area on a violent wind storm.

FORESTS ARE NO FINAL FIX

7 March 2006 ～

Many years ago, the poet Edna St Vincent Millay wrote a little ditty which might aptly describe our current addiction to the burning of fossil fuels:

My candle burns at both ends;
  It will not last the night;
But, ah, my foes, and oh, my friends –
  It gives a lovely light!

The two ends of this particular candle, as we know, are the finite availability of the fossil fuels themselves on the one hand, and the carbon dioxide waste pumped into the atmosphere by burning the remaining stocks, with adverse consequences for the global climate. The notion might occur to some, however, that we could solve at least the second of these problems by applying National Tree Week strategy on a global scale.

As happens every year, during the current National Tree Week 2006, some 15,000 trees are being distributed by Coillte for planting by a wide variety of community groups, schools and clubs of every kind around the country. But could we not solve the global warming problem in its entirety by adopting this strategy on a global scale? Could we not plant sufficient trees to gobble up all the extra carbon dioxide emitted by the burning of fossil fuels?

Well, it has been thought about. Fossil fuel combustion at present exudes an extra six billion tonnes or thereabouts of CO_2 into the Earth's atmosphere every year. How much carbon a single tree *extracts*, on the other hand, is difficult to calculate, and in any case varies depending on the age of the tree and on other environmental parameters at the time. It has been estimated, however, that the European Union's family of forests extracts somewhere between 100 and 300 million tons of CO_2 per year, and also that a young plantation of, say, sycamore trees in temperate latitudes absorbs an annual quota of some 7.5 tonnes for every hectare.

Based on figures like these, the necessary area to be planted with trees to extract the fossil fuel carbon would be somewhere in the region of seven million square kilometres, or an area roughly equivalent to the continent of Australia. If this sounds unachievable—which it is, of course, in practical terms—it is a sobering thought that the required seven million square kilometres corresponds almost exactly to the area of tropical forest estimated to have been removed by humans for agricultural activities during the past 10,000 years.

In any event, such a solution would be only temporary. Trees assimilate carbon dioxide fastest when they are young, and the uptake slows down significantly as an area of forestry matures. Some older forests, indeed, whether because of forest fires or of plant diseases killing off the trees, become net contributors of CO_2. And sooner or later all timber, no matter the use to which it may be put, must ultimately decay, and its carbon be assimilated back into the global system.

A LITTLE HELP FROM SOME HEAVEN

11 *March* 2006 ～

Yesterday we had yet another feastday, that of the Forty Martyrs of Sebaste. In the context of their times, there is nothing terribly remarkable about the fate of the Forty Martyrs; they were Christians executed for their faith in that Armenian city around AD320, a common enough occurrence in the domain of Constantine's then co-emperor, Licinius. The devout forty, however, were soldiers of the *Legio Fulminata*, the so-called 'Thunder Legion', the derivation of whose name is of some meteorological significance.

The story goes back a century and a half to when the Roman emperor Marcus Aurelius was engaged in a war against the Quadi, a tribe on the northern borders of the empire in what is now Slovakia. On one occasion in AD172, Marcus's armies were encircled and their situation was very bleak indeed. The Greek historian Cassius Dio takes up the story:

> The barbarians would not give them battle, in hopes of their perishing by heat and thirst, since they had so surrounded them that they had no possible means of getting water. And when they were in the utmost distress from sickness, sun and thirst, and could neither fight nor retreat, suddenly clouds gathered, and a copious rain fell. The Romans, raising their mouths towards heaven, received it upon them, and next, turning up their shields and helmets, drank largely out of them, and gave to their horses.
>
> Then a violent hail-storm and much lightning were discharged upon the enemy. And thus water and fire might be

seen in the same place falling from heaven, that some might drink refreshment, and others be burned to death; for the fire did not touch the Romans.

And so, ultimately, the Romans were victorious.

Now, there seems to be no doubt about the historical occurrence of this crucial thunderstorm, but there are diverse opinions on its source. On the Antonine Column in Rome, the 'miracle of the thunderstorm' is represented as wrought by Jupiter. According to Cassius Dio, on the other hand, 'Harnuphis, an Egyptian magician, who was a companion of Marcus, invoked by means of enchantments various deities and in particular Mercury, the god of the air, and by this means attracted the rain.'

The Christian tradition handed down by Tertullian, however, has it that the besieged emperor was told by one of his officers that 'those who are called Christians can accomplish anything whatever by their prayers, and that in the army there chanced to be a whole division of this sect. Marcus, on hearing this, appealed to them to pray to their God.' When the partisan thunderstorm arrived and saved the day, 'Marcus was greatly astonished, and to the Twelfth Legion he gave the surname *fulminata*, that is, "thundering".'

History, disappointingly, records that the *Legio XII Fulminata* had been known by that name for more than a century before this incident.

A DAY AND A YEAR TO REMEMBER

15 March 2006 ∿

'**M**any report', writes Plutarch in his *Parallel Lives*, 'that a certain soothsayer forewarned Caesar of great danger threatening him on the Ides of March. When the day was come, as he was going to the Senate House Caesar called out to the soothsayer and said laughingly: "The Ides of March are come"; to which the soothsayer answered softly, "Yes, Caesar, but not gone".'

Pedestrian stuff, of course, compared to Shakespeare's brilliant and durable translation to the stage of the dramatic events of 15 March 44 BC. It was Shakespeare's rendering, based on Plutarch, of Julius Caesar's unfortunate experience under Pompey's statue on that fateful day which gave the Ides of March its memorable ring, and indeed it is the only date of the old Roman calendar still commonly remembered.

They were strange times those, around the time of Caesar's death. We can take with a pinch of salt, I suppose, Horatio's story in *Hamlet* that:

> *In the most high and palmy state of Rome,*
> *A little ere the mightiest Julius fell,*
> *The graves stood tenantless, and the sheeted dead*
> *Did squeak and gibber in the Roman streets.*

But we might look more seriously at Casca's comment to Cicero in *Julius Caesar* before the big event:

I have seen tempests, when the scolding winds
Have rived the knotty oaks . . .
But never till to-night, never till now,
Did I go through a tempest dropping fire.

It does seem that around the time of Caesar's assassination, and right through the following summer of 44BC, the Roman weather was very unusual indeed. Again, Plutarch tells us that 'there were earthquakes and obscurations of the Sun's rays, and during all that year its orb rose pale and without radiance and the fruits, imperfect and half ripe, withered away and shrivelled up on account of the coldness of the atmosphere'.

Virgil tells much the same story in his familiar style:

Ille etiam extincto miseratus Cæsare Romam,
Cum caput obscura nitidum ferrugine texit,

or as our own Peter Fallon translates it in his *Georgics of Virgil*:

And it was he [the Sun] *who felt for Rome that time*
    that Caesar fell
and veiled his gleaming head in gloom
so dark the infidels began to fear that night would last
    forever.

A few lines further on, however, Virgil and Fallon provide a clue to what has happened:

How frequently we've watched eruptions of Mount
    Etna
and the expulsions from her furnaces spill on the one-
    eyed giants' lands
fireballs and molten lava.

Etna, clearly, was in eruptive mood in 44BC; a veil of dust obscured the normally radiant Italian Sun and the volcano's rumblings affected Roman weather in diverse other ways.

TOO COLD FOR SNOW?

18 *March* 2006 ～

'This place is too cold for hell,' says Shakespeare's Porter of Macbeth's castle at Inverness. We have had some inkling of his frame of mind in recent days, with flurries of snow here and there to complete the wintry picture. But could it ever be 'too cold for snow', as is oftentimes suggested?

The short answer is 'No'; it is too warm for it when the air temperature is above 4°C or thereabouts, but in general it is never too cold for it to snow. That having been said, however, there are several atmospheric processes at work to decrease the *intensity* of snowfall when the temperature drops significantly below the zero mark.

Firstly, the lower the temperature, the less moisture the air can hold in the form of water vapour; consequently, when the atmosphere is very cold, it has less water available for precipitation of any kind than when the temperature is higher. And secondly, ice crystals in a cloud tend to grow in size most rapidly when they have as yet unfrozen water droplets to combine with. At very low temperatures, however, there are no unfrozen water droplets, and so individual ice crystals grow in size only comparatively slowly. Moreover, the largest snowflakes occur when the air temperature at the surface is just slightly above zero. It is then cold enough for the snow to survive to reach the ground in solid form, but the individual crystals are slightly wet and therefore adhere together easily to form the complex and varied patterns of the familiar snowflake. But at very low temperatures this does not happen, and such precipitation as may occur will comprise only a light sprinkling of tiny crystals.

The same conditions that favour large snowflakes also produce snow that is good for snowballs. To form a snowball, it is necessary for the flakes to cling together. In the process of making the snowball, hand compression causes sharp increases in pressure near the pointed ends of the ice crystals, and this in turn, when the snow is not too cold, causes localised melting to take place. Then, when the pressure is removed, the melted water freezes again and glues neighbouring crystals together to produce a nice firm snowball. In very cold snow, however, as often found in Scandinavia and on the Continent, this useful temporary melting, and therefore the subsequent refreezing which cements the ball, does not normally take place.

But perhaps the most relevant reason for the myth that it may sometimes be 'too cold for snow' is the fact that in these parts the very lowest temperatures usually occur on clear, frosty winter nights when the ground loses heat by long-wave radiation out to space. In these very cold—and usually anticyclonic—conditions, there is no snow simply because there are no clouds around in which any snow might form.

TWO BRIGHT STARS OF MATHEMATICS

24 *March* 2006 ✺

There has been much ado in recent months about Sir William Rowan Hamilton, Ireland's most distinguished mathematician, who was simultaneously Director of Dunsink Observatory, Andrews Professor of Astronomy at Trinity College, and Astronomer Royal of Ireland, all from 1827 until 1865. One of his successors to these offices, however, although less well known, was a man of comparable distinction.

Edmund Taylor Whittaker was born in Lancashire in October 1873. A brilliant student of mathematics at Cambridge University, he went on to publish several standards works on various aspects of the subject while only in his twenties; he was also an outstanding lecturer, later described by one of his pupils as having 'a curious mixture of precision and grace, always moving with deceptive ease through the subject and making it at once a logical structure and a work of art'.

Although he had no experience of practical astronomy, Whittaker's reputation as a mathematician was sufficient to bring about his appointment to Dunsink in 1906 at the age of thirty-two. During his six-year term of office, he organised the refurbishment of much of the equipment, and introduced important innovations in the field of photographic photometry—the technique of using objective photographic methods to measure the brightness, or magnitude, of stars, which had previously been done subjectively. In 1912, Whittaker left Dunsink to take up a professorship at Edinburgh University, where he remained until his death.

But perhaps the most remarkable outcome of Whittaker's sojourn at Dunsink was the friendship that developed between him and the future Taoiseach, Éamon de Valera. When Whittaker arrived in Ireland, de Valera was professor of mathematics at Our Lady's Training College in Carysfort, Blackrock. Dev attended Whittaker's lectures on mathematics and in November 1908 Whittaker gave his protégé the following reference: 'Mr Edward de Valera has attended several of my Professorial Courses of lectures on Spectroscopy, Astrophysics, and Electro-Optics during the past two years. In the personal intercourse which has thus been brought about, I have been much impressed by the intellectual vigour with which he has interested himself in the most difficult problems of Natural Philosophy. His knowledge is both broad and deep, and I am confident that in any educational position he will exercise the best influences over those with whom he is brought into contact.'

Their friendship continued over five decades, and it was to Whittaker that de Valera turned for advice on the establishment of the Dublin Institute for Advanced Studies. Indeed it was envisaged that Whittaker would accept a Senior Professorship at the Institute, which came into being in June 1940, but the war prevented this from happening.

Sir Edmund Whittaker was received into the Catholic Church in 1930 and became in due course a member of the select Pontifical Academy. He was knighted in 1945, and died in Edinburgh 50 years ago today, on 24 March 1956.

TIME FOR A LITANY OF ANSWERS

25 March 2006 ∽

I had a nice email from a gentleman the other day, and he posed a litany of questions. They related to the twice-yearly oscillation of our clocks from GMT to 'Summer Time' and *vice versa*, and since one such lurch takes place in the small hours of tomorrow morning, it seems appropriate today to try to give some answers. The questions were: What are the origins of changing the clocks? Is it always one hour? Does every country in the world do this? Do they all change the same weekend? Didn't we experiment with different timings in the 1970s and revert? Why do the clocks change in Ireland in the last weekends of March and October, since a change, for example, in the first weekend of March would give tourists and gardeners much longer evenings?

Let's take them one by one. Benjamin Franklin, in 1780, is credited with being the first to come up with the notion of 'Daylight Saving Time'. No one thought about it much, however, until the early twentieth century, when one William Willett, a wealthy builder from Chelsea, had more or less the same idea; it occurred to him that everyone in Britain got out of bed too late during the summer months, thereby shortening the time available for outdoor recreation in the evening, and he suggested four successive 20-minute advances of the clock as spring turned into summer.

Again, no one took much notice until World War I, when on 31 March 1916 the Germans advanced their clocks by an hour in the interests of economy and productivity. When Austria followed suit, and then the Netherlands, Willett's ideas began to make more sense, and the measure was quickly enacted into British, and therefore Irish, law. The 'Spring forward—Fall back' idea has been with us, with some variations, ever since.

Daylight Saving Time is a creature of the higher latitudes. Near the equator there is little difference in effective daylight through the year, so a change in time would serve no purpose. Outside the tropics, however, the practice is almost universal—usually at a weekend, but not always at the same weekend. In recent years the change has taken place simultaneously in all countries of the EU; other nations make their own arrangements, but always around the same time of year.

From 1968 to 1971, GMT was abandoned in Britain and Ireland, and our clocks stayed one hour ahead of Greenwich throughout the year, but the dark winter mornings were unpopular, and the experiment was abandoned. And as to the asymmetry of the change around the winter solstice—the fact that the period from late October to the solstice is much shorter than from the solstice to late March—I have to confess that, despite much searching, I have never found a convincing explanation.

| THE SIGNS OF A RED SKY

27 *March* 2006 ∽

P robably the best-known weather saying of all time is that about the colour of the sky at sunrise and sunset, which in its most popular version goes:

Red sky at night is the shepherd's delight,
Red sky in the morning is the shepherd's warning.

It has been around in one guise or another for thousands of years. The Greek philosopher Theophrastus, for example, quoted it at length: 'The plainest sign of rain', he said, 'is that which is to be observed in the morning, when the sky appears to be reddened over before the Sun rises.' Another ancient Greek, Aratus, invoked Aurora, the goddess of the dawn, to illustrate the same morning phenomenon, albeit with an optimistic slant:

> Or if Aurora tinge with glowing red
> The clouds that float round Phoebus's rising head,
> Farmer, rejoice! For soon refreshing rains
> Will fill the pools and quench the thirsty plains.

And then he went on to be equally optimistic about a red Sun in the evening:

> If with clear face in his watery bed,
> Curtained with crimson clouds around his head,
> He sink, that night no rain or tempest fear;
> And tomorrow's Sun will shine serene and clear.

It was a popular portent even in biblical times since, according to St Matthew, the Lord reminded the Pharisees that 'When it is evening, ye say it will be fair weather for the sky is red; and in the morning, it will be foul weather today because the sky is red and lowring'.

But is there any sense in all this nonsense? Meteorologists, being cautious folk, will hedge their bets and say it all depends. They will warn you first that there are different shades of evening red. There is the deep crimson, angry red, which indicates an excess of water vapour in the air and augurs ill; and there is the gentle yellowish pink or rose-coloured tint of sunlight being filtered through a dry atmosphere, which may indeed be taken, as Shakespeare puts it, as a 'token of a goodly day tomorrow'.

A red sky in the morning, however, is much less dependable. If the redness is in the east in the neighbourhood of the rising Sun, it may well be that the rain-bearing and westward-moving clouds have passed us by, and the rest of the day, contrary to the wisdom of the rhyme, may well be fine. But if, on the other hand, the *western* sky is a lurid, angry red, an approaching rain front may be acting as a screen on to which the rising Sun has cast colours; then it may well turn out to be a rainy day.

THE COINCIDENTAL PERFECTION OF A SOLAR ECLIPSE

28 *March* 2006 ~

Eclipses, like sorrows to Shakespeare's king of Denmark, come rarely as single spies but in battalions. Well, perhaps not quite battalions, but often as two or three together over a small number of weeks. So it was that we had a penumbral eclipse of the Moon two weeks ago, and tomorrow an eclipse of the Sun is predicted to occur. There was a time when such happenings boded ill, as Gloucester tells us in *King Lear*: 'These late eclipses in the Sun and Moon portend no good to us; love cools, friendship falls off, brothers divide; in cities, mutinies; in countries, discord; in palaces, treason; and the bond cracked 'twixt son and father.' But nowadays we view them with more equanimity.

A solar eclipse occurs when the Moon passes directly between our planet and the Sun. It obscures for a time our view of the solar disc, or viewed from space, the Moon casts a shadow on the surface of the Earth. Since the Moon is tiny by comparison, the shadow is only very small, a circle of darkness about 100 miles in diameter that skims rapidly from west to east across the landscape.

Tomorrow's eclipse will be seen in the full glory of its totality only along a narrow strip that runs from Brazil across Africa and Turkey, and then in between the Black and Caspian Seas into the plains of Asia. A partial eclipse, however, will be visible over a much wider zone; here in Ireland the Moon will obscure about 15 to 20 per cent of the solar disc between 11am and 12 noon.

The fact that a total eclipse can occur at all is due to a strange astronomical coincidence. The Sun is about 400 times bigger than our Moon, but because it is also around 400 times farther away from us, the two bodies appear in the sky as almost identical in size—a fact that can be verified by the even most casual observer of the skies. As a result, during an eclipse, the Moon covers the whole Sun, but only just. Earth is the only planet in our galaxy where a 'perfect eclipse' like this occurs; at the last count there were something like 150 moons of various sizes in the solar system, and in all cases their apparent size, as viewed from their parent planets, is either so big that it totally obscures the Sun, or too small to cover the solar disc.

Neither was it always so on Earth. Our Moon probably started out as a lump of molten material blasted from Earth by some celestial collision some four billion years ago. Since then it has been gradually receding from the Earth, and the right distance for a perfect eclipse was reached only 150 million years ago, almost yesterday in the language of cosmology.

THE COGITATIONS OF ONE RENÉ DESCARTES

31 *March* 2006 ∾

L e bon sens, wrote René Descartes, *est la chose du monde la mieux partagée, car chacun pense en être bien pourvu*: 'Common sense must be the best distributed commodity around, since everyone is convinced that he or she is well supplied with it.'

Descartes was born in La Haye in France 410 years ago today, on 31 March 1596, at an interesting time in the history of meteorology. For 2,000 years the science had been one of speculation based on preconceived ideas, almost entirely those written down by Aristotle. Descartes, however—and not without controversy—broke with this tradition and challenged many of the Aristotelian notions; he applied his own deductive reasoning to the world about him, and rejected many of the time-honoured and accepted explanations of everyday weather events.

It was Descartes, for example, who in 1637 was the first to provide a convincing account of the optical processes that make up the rainbow. Moreover, although Evangelista Torricelli is generally credited with the invention of the barometer in 1643, it was Descartes who subsequently conceived the idea of using simultaneous pressure readings to analyse weather patterns.

Descartes did his best to put this latter theory to the test. The earliest meteorological observations of which records remain were made between 1649 and 1651, around the same time in Paris and Clermont-Ferrand in France, and in Stockholm in Sweden. The first of these, the Swedish set of observations, were made by René Descartes.

But, most famously, it was Descartes in his book *Le Discours de la Methode* who came to the singular conclusion that *Cogito, ergo sum.* 'Considering', he wrote, 'that the very thoughts we have while we are awake may also occur while we sleep without any of them being at that time true, I resolved to pretend that all the things that had ever entered my mind were no more true than the illusions of my dreams. But immediately I noticed that, while I was trying thus to think everything false, it was necessary that I, who was thinking this, was something. And observing that this truth "I am thinking, therefore I exist" was so firm and sure that all the most extravagant suppositions of the sceptics were incapable of shaking it, I decided that I could accept it without scruple as the first principle of the philosophy I sought.'

Although born in France, Descartes spent most of his working life in Holland. Then in 1649 he was summoned to Stockholm by Queen Christina, a passionate and learned lady who demanded daily lessons from him at five o'clock each morning. The unaccustomed early rising and the bitter Scandinavian winter were too much for Descartes; he contracted the pneumonia from which he died in February 1650.

A BRIEF, CONSPICUOUS, BUT ULTIMATELY GENTLE TURBULENCE

1 *April* 2006 ∾

'There were many days of wind and rain. Uneasy gusts ruffled the surface of the lake, sending it running this way and that. Occasionally, a rainbow arched all the way across the lake. More often the rainbows were as broken as the weather, appearing here and there in streaks or brilliant patches of colour in the unsettled sky. When rain wasn't dripping from the leaves or eaves, the air was so heavy it was like breathing rain.'

That the weather is that of the Irish midlands will be evident to all, but only connoisseurs, perhaps, may recognise the unique, understated style of the late John McGahern. His last novel, *That They May Face the Rising Sun*, had an ambience that differed greatly from that of many of his earlier works. Novels like *The Barracks* and *The Dark* explored the troubled, less happy side of Irish life but his finale was a celebration of the inherent goodness, often deliberately and self-consciously disguised, to be found in the innocent, rural communities typical of not too long ago.

There are other examples in the book of McGahern's gentle touch when evoking atmosphere by reference to the weather. For example, when the year has reached high summer, he describes the sudden agitation of one of his protagonists as,

. . . like the eruptions of air that occur in the wheaten light of mown meadows in a heatwave. Dried grass and leaves, and even bits of stick, are sent whirling high in a noisy, spinning cylinder of dust and violent air, which then as quickly dies, to reappear like a mirage in another part of the meadow.

Dust devils—for it is one of these McGahern describes—are small-scale whirlwinds which sometimes develop on hot, sunny, almost windless days. Heated by the sun-baked soil, a small volume of air may become warmer than its environment and start to rise. Soon a vigorous but very localised updraft develops, the air ascending in an accelerating spiral, carrying aloft any dust, litter, hay or straw it may encounter.

Unlike tornadoes, dust devils are not associated with thundery shower clouds. Indeed they are most likely to form when the sky is virtually clear, allowing the Sun free rein to heat an arid landscape. The dust-whirls are limited in their size and intensity by the dryness of the local atmosphere, since if the air had more moisture it would condense in the spiralling updraft and contribute extra energy in the form of 'latent heat of condensation' to an embryonic storm. But in very dry conditions, only the energy provided by the initial heating is available; it is soon exhausted, and the whirlwind dies.

Is there hidden, I wonder, in the lifecycle of this brief, conspicuous, but ultimately gentle turbulence, a metaphor for the life of John McGahern himself?

THE WEATHER SETS THE SCENE

10 *April* 2006 ～

The weather is a useful tool for novelists. Sunshine, for example, conveys a mood of optimistic cheerfulness, while a depressing atmosphere is called up by introducing fog or rain. Extreme heat, on the other hand, provokes irritation, lust or jealousies, which may well result in climactic violence in a cathartic thunderstorm. Heavy showers bring sheltering protagonists together in close, intimate surroundings, while gales or blizzards can remove superfluous characters from the scene completely.

Evelyn Waugh, who died 40 years ago today, on 10 April 1966, was a master of such meteorological manipulation. In his best-known work, *Brideshead Revisited*, the elements subtly reinforce the moods prevailing at the time.

The Sun shines continuously, for example, during the first golden episodes in Oxford as Charles Ryder is entrained into the surreal, ephemeral world of plover's eggs and vintage breakfast wines, and becomes entranced in his whirlwind friendship with Sebastian. But as Charles, even while still at Oxford, becomes emotionally entangled with the aristocratic and dysfunctional Flytes, the atmosphere and the weather wax more sombre:

Everywhere, on cobble and gravel and lawn, the leaves were falling, and in the College gardens the smoke of the bonfires joined the river mist, drifting across the grey walls; the flags were oily underfoot and as, one by one, the lamps were lit in the windows round the quad, the golden lights were diffuse and remote. The autumnal mood possessed us both, as though the riotous exuberance of June had died with the gillyflowers, whose scent at my windows now yielded to the damp leaves, smouldering in a corner of the quad.

Years later when Charles and Julia, Sebastian's sister, fall in love in mid-Atlantic, the dark, mysterious forces that will ultimately wreck their doomed relationship are epitomised in the powerful storm that forms the backdrop. And sometimes, too, like many of the characters, the weather is not exactly what it seems: Lord Marchmain on his deathbed, immersed in his own dark winter of the soul, believes it to be wintertime outside, being 'oblivious of the deep corn and swelling fruit and the surfeited bees who slowly sought their hives in the heavy, afternoon sunlight outside his windows'.

Charles and Julia plan to marry, divorcing their respective spouses, but ultimately Julia yields to the pervasive influence of the Roman Church, and the lovers part forever. 'I stood at a window in the drawing-room,' Charles recalls, 'watching the wind at work stripping the lime trees, sweeping down the yellow leaves, sweeping along the terrace and lawns, trailing them through puddles and over the wet grass, pasting them on walls and window-panes, leaving them at length in sodden piles against the stonework.' As Ryder contemplates the bleakness of his future, the elements themselves reflect his helplessness against the manipulating forces that have brought about his plight.

AN EYE ON THE PACIFIC

11 *April* 2006 ～

Many weatherpeople these days resemble

> *. . . stout Cortez, when with eagle eyes,*
> *He stared at the Pacific—and all his men*
> *Looked at each other with a wild surmise—*
> *Silent upon a peak in Darien.*

The focus of their meteorological concentration is the temperature of the surface waters of that great ocean; it seems to be slightly lower than usual, which suggests that another La Niña episode may have just begun.

La Niña is the *alter ego* of El Niño. The latter, as we know, is an occasional warming for a year or two of the surface waters of the Pacific over a broad band in the low latitudes straddling the equator; it occurs every three to seven years. This warmer water over a vast expanse of ocean might be compared to shovelling extra coal into the great firebox of the global atmospheric engine, and it affects the world's climate. At the peak of a strong El Niño episode, normally arid areas of western South America are drenched with rain, and other low-latitude regions, like Indonesia and parts of Northern Australia where rain is normally abundant, experience severe droughts and their attendant hardships.

But El Niño—literally 'the boy child'—has a little sister who, although more retiring and subject to less publicity, presents with her own symptoms of disturbed behaviour. La Niña is the name given to episodes when the surface waters of the tropical Pacific are *colder* than they ought to be, and it imprints its own particular signature—almost a mirror image of El Niño—on the global weather. Places which suffer droughts during an El Niño experience prolonged torrential downpours when La Niña comes—and *vice versa.*

The swings and roundabouts of El Niño and La Niña also complicate the detection of climatic change. The anomalies in global temperature and rainfall patterns which they bring about have to be eliminated before any underlying trends can be identified, a problem made more difficult by the fact that the pair come and go at irregular intervals, and with an intensity that is different every time.

The La Niña just beginning is predicted to be weak. It will be watched with interest, however, because the El Niño/La Niña cycle is known to affect the frequency and intensity of hurricanes in the North Atlantic; hurricanes tend to be fewer and weaker during an El Niño, and *vice versa* with La Niña. The last few years, on the other hand, although clearly in the El Niño sector of the cycle, have been marked by very active hurricane seasons; now with La Niña appearing on the scene, meteorologists will watch with interest, perhaps even trepidation, to see if it results in 2006 being an even more eventful year for Caribbean/North Atlantic storms than the quite spectacular 2005.

COLD SPELLS AND BRIGHT IDEAS

13 *April* 2006 ◡

The sun was warm but the wind was chill;
You know how it is with an April day.

Robert Frost defined the problem; Alexander Buchan provided an explanation—or so, at least, some thought.

Buchan was a Scot who carried out a detailed statistical study of weather in his native Scotland in the 1860s. He was no eccentric dilettante; he was one of the foremost meteorologists of his day, for more than 40 years the presiding genius of the Scottish Meteorological Society, and in a famous paper in 1867 called *Interruptions in the Regular Rise and Fall of Temperature in the Course of the Year*, he concluded that certain periods of the year were significantly colder or warmer than they ought to be.

Buchan identified six cold periods and three unseasonably warm ones. The warm spells were 12–15 July, 12–15 August, and 3–14 December; and the cold spells were 7–14 February, 11–14 April, 9–14 May, 29 June to 4 July, 6–11 August, and 6–13 November. As can be seen, the current rather chilly conditions coincide closely with Buchan's second allegedly cold period near the middle of April.

As it happens, meteorologists nowadays treat 'Buchan's Spells', as they are called, with scepticism. In the first place, even Buchan himself was aware that his studies referred only to Scotland, and that there was no reason to suppose that they should apply elsewhere. In any case, more sophisticated statistical analyses over longer periods have not supported Buchan's findings.

But for some years Buchan Spells gained considerable currency and were widely quoted. Indeed some 20 years after Buchan died in 1907, his theories were at the centre of a political controversy when Lord Desborough had the bright idea that there would be many advantages to having Easter, like all our other major holidays, at a fixed time every year; he proposed the first Sunday after the second Saturday in April, or in effect, between the 9th and the 15th.

The arguments in favour of the reform were many and cogent; it was widely admitted that the existing vagaries of the chief festival in the Christian year were ill-founded and inconvenient.

Even from an ecclesiastical viewpoint, the period specified was seen as good; it would mean that the new Easter could never depart by more than a few days from what was believed to have been the actual date of the Resurrection.

Unfortunately, an obscure official of the Royal Meteorological Society, theretofore and ever since unknown, spotted that the proposed dates corresponded closely with Buchan's cold spell in mid-April. Although Lord Desborough's Bill was formally enacted, the prospect of a chilly Easter in perpetuity proved too much for the Great British Public to endure; following many angry letters to *The Times*, the bright idea was never implemented.

THE GOSPEL ACCORDING TO VAN EYCK

14 April 2006 ~

'And when the sixth hour was come, there was darkness over the whole land until the ninth hour.' So says St Mark in his account of the events being commemorated today around the world, and since both Matthew and Luke describe the phenomenon in almost identical words, we must assume its meteorological plausibility.

The practice of dividing the day into twenty-four equal hours did not come into common use until the late Middle Ages. Throughout the Roman Empire, time was reckoned in 'temporal hours', a system whereby both the day and night were separately divided into twelve equal intervals. Daytime hours in summer were therefore longer than in winter; at the summer solstice in Rome, for example, the day comprised twelve 76-minute hours and the night twelve 44-minute hours. The *ninth* hour, when according to Mark 'Jesus yielded up the ghost', would have been this number of temporal hours from sunrise on that first Good Friday, a time which better minds than mine have reckoned to be about three o'clock in the afternoon.

The Crucifixion in the New York Metropolitan Museum of Art is attributed to the Flemish painter Jan van Eyck (c.1385–1441), and is by far the most meteorologically interesting portrayal of these great events. It not only contains an accurate depiction of almost every common type of cloud, but also, fortuitously or not, hints at a possible explanation for the interval of relative darkness.

The scene is the familiar one. It shows a large crowd around the three crosses on Mount Calvary, and captures the instant when the side of Christ is lanced by the spear of one of the assembled soldiers. The sky progresses from a deep, deep blue around the zenith to a milky white as the eye approaches the horizon, a precise portrayal of the range of shading clearly visible in the real sky in clear conditions. The main cloud type is clearly recognisable as cumulus, showing the characteristic scalloped edges and the rounded tops; elsewhere, a long stream of cirrus clouds slopes gently downwards from the centre of the sky, and above the cirrus is another patch of cloud that resembles cirrocumulus. Near the upper left-hand corner altocumulus lenticularis, or mountain-wave cloud, is clearly to be seen.

From the astronomical information available—the proximity to the Passover, the waning gibbous Moon and the putative position of an afternoon Sun—it may be deduced that the observer faces towards the north. Moreover, the characteristic clouds, together with three windmills facing northeast to define the direction of the wind, allow us to conclude that a cold front has probably passed the scene an hour or two before, and cleared the sky. Could it have been the heavy clouds associated with this cold front, according to van Eyck, that caused the three-hour period of unnatural gloom a little time before?

| MOVING SUNS AND STATUES

15 *April* 2006 ～

Have you noticed that the eccentric oscillations of our rural statues have been strangely still of late? As it happens, they have their counterpart in the folklore of other countries where it is believed—or was believed in bygone times— that the Sun dances on an Easter Sunday morning.

One John Evans, for example, writing in the seventeenth century, recalls how he 'went up a hill to see the Easter Sun appear, and saw it rise, skip, play, dance and turn about like a whale'. Likewise the English poet John Suckling, around the same time, alludes to the phenomenon while contemplating the terpsichorean perfection of his lady friend:

> *But oh, she dances such a way;*
> *No sun upon an Easter day*
> *Is half so fine a sight.*

Meteorologists would argue that both Johns were under an illusion—at least in their observations of the Easter Sun.

It all goes back to the nature of the feast itself. Easter is named after Eostre, the pagan goddess of the dawn, to whom a sacrifice was made around the vernal equinox. Long after such sacrifices were abandoned, it remained the custom to rise early on Easter morning to observe the dawn, and as in the case of the moving statues, minds concentrated on the rising Sun imagined things they did not really see.

When the Sun is low in the sky, its rays must travel a very long distance through the Earth's atmosphere to reach an observer, and refraction or 'bending' of the light beams sometimes results in unusual optical effects. Under certain atmospheric conditions the Sun may assume strange shapes: it may resemble a loaf of bread, a mushroom, or a fish—or even appear to be divided into two or more parts. These optical changes sometimes follow one another in quick succession, and with the help of a little imagination, it was not difficult for our ancestors to believe that the Easter Sun was indeed dancing on the horizon.

But another gentleman of the seventeenth century, Sir Thomas Browne, put the matter in perspective in his *Pseudodoxia Epidemica*, or *Vulgar Errors*, published in 1646: 'We shall not, I hope, disparage the Resurrection of our Redeemer, if we say the Sun doth *not* dance on Easter day. And though we would willingly assent to any sympathetical exultation, we cannot conceive therein any more than a Tropical expression.'

With this dismissal Sir Thomas was not, as you might think, suggesting that the phenomenon was peculiar to the lower latitudes, but rather that it had its origins in a *trope*—words used in a metaphorical or figurative sense. 'Whether any such motion were there on the day that Christ arised,' he concluded sensibly, 'Scripture hath not revealed, which hath been very punctual in other records concerning solary miracles.'

A RADICAL OBSERVER OF THE WEATHER

17 *April* 2006 ∾

William Molyneux of Dublin was an unlikely antecedent to those whose controversial activities we commemorated this weekend. Yet, *mutatis mutandis* to take account of different times, Molyneux's *The Case of Ireland's being bound by Acts of Parliament in England* has much in common with their various promulgations. This nationalistic declaration created a sensation in its day, and attracted sufficient attention for it to be condemned by the Westminster parliament as being 'of dangerous tendency to the Crown and to the people of England'.

'If the religion, lives, liberties, fortunes, and estates of the clergy, nobility and gentry of Ireland', wrote Molyneux, 'may be disposed of without their privity or consent, what benefit have they of any laws, liberties, or privileges granted to them by the crown of England? I am loth to give their condition an hard name; but I have no other notion of slavery than being bound by a law to which I do not consent.'

Molyneux, however, was far from being a revolutionary. He was born into a distinguished Anglo-Irish family of French extraction 350 years ago today, on 17 April 1656, and educated at Trinity College before studying law in London. For the rest of his life, he lived in Dublin, which in the closing years of Charles II's reign was a pleasing city for the comfortable classes. War and tension in the time of Cromwell had been succeeded by a period of prosperity and peace; the city had grown rapidly, spreading far beyond its mediaeval boundaries and trebling in population to around 60,000 souls by 1685. A man of culture with a taste for philosophy and science might find many places worse in which to live.

And William Molyneux had a taste for both. He was a friend and confidante of the philosopher John Locke, many of whose ideas were incorporated into *The Case of Ireland . . .*; and in the realm of science, Molyneux is remembered as the man who compiled the first series of scientific weather observations in this country.

His lifetime was an era of rapid development in scientific instruments, and Molyneux and others of his ilk were quick to appreciate their potential for gaining an insight into the behaviour of the atmosphere. In March 1684 he began a 'Weather Register' at Trinity College which for the first time in Ireland included readings of barometric pressure, and by 2 June that year he had compiled enough material to present a paper on his findings to the Dublin Society. The series of observations was continued by Molyneux and others for a little over two years, from 1684 to 1686, and although only a small fragment of it still survives, preserved in the Bodleian Library in Oxford, it is nonetheless regarded as one of the most important milestones in the history of Irish meteorology.

CENTENARY OF A CATASTROPHE

18 *April* 2006 ∿

Three great natural disasters in American history dwarf all others in terms of loss of life and property. The most lethal occurred on 8 September 1900, when a major hurricane scored a direct hit on Galveston Island on the Texas coast of the Gulf of Mexico; it destroyed 3,600 houses and killed nearly 8,000 people, about a sixth of the island's entire population. Eleven years previously more than 2,000 citizens of Johnstown, Pennsylvania, perished following the rupture of a dam on the Conemaugh River after several days of heavy rain in May 1889. But the best remembered natural disaster to strike the North American continent was the San Francisco earthquake of 18 April 1906, a century ago today.

Although usually referred to as the 'San Francisco' earthquake, the tremor was in fact felt right along the entire length of the San Andreas fault. This fault runs for some 300 miles along the Californian coast, and since its formation 150 million years ago, its opposite sides have moved with respect to each other a total distance of some 300 miles. The particular movement which caused the earthquake of 1906 accounted for some 20 feet of this displacement, but the San Andreas runs right through the suburbs of San Francisco, and this being the centre of greatest population, was also the scene of greatest devastation.

The earthquake began quietly enough just after 5am, but built up to a fierce crescendo over a period of about forty seconds. The noise was deafening; superimposed on the frightful roar of the 'quake itself, and the sound of breaking glass and falling buildings, was the weird cacophony of church bells, jangling insanely as their belfries swayed. Then the racket stopped suddenly.

But as Wordsworth says:

> *All things have second birth;*
> *The earthquake is not satisfied at once.*

After a ten-second respite, the furore began again, this time even more violently, and continued for a further 30 seconds. These major tremors were followed by many smaller earthquakes—the aftershocks—but none of these was serious.

Many of the older wooden-framed houses and buildings were able to absorb the shock more pliantly than structures made of steel or stone, and consequently suffered less immediate damage. They were no match, however, for the ensuing fires, caused by blocked chimneys and overturned stoves, which quickly took hold over what was left of the city during the next three days.

At the final count 450 lives were lost, and 3,500 persons seriously injured; thirty schools, eighty churches and the homes of 250,000 people were demolished; the six-million-dollar City Hall, the pride of San Francisco, was a total wreck; and 2,800 acres were razed by fire, including the entire business and financial centre of the city. The damage was estimated at $250m, in today's terms close to a billion US dollars.

THE UNPREDICTABLE BLUE DANUBE

19 *April* 2006 ~

The immediate causes of the present Danube flooding are not difficult to find. A complex area of low pressure over the region in recent weeks produced prolonged thundery downpours of rain; these, combined with melt-water from the superabundant snow which so delighted skiers in central European highlands during the winter months, have resulted in more water being to hand than the river can comfortably accommodate. But there are other underlying reasons, too.

The spectre of climate change always lurks in the background to such happenings these days. We cannot with confidence, of course, assign any individual incident like this to global warming, but the crisis is consistent with an emerging greenhouse world. Higher temperatures mean more evaporation, and therefore ultimately more moisture in the atmosphere to fall as rain.

The Intergovernmental Panel on Climate Change concluded in its most recent report in 2001 that 'in the middle and high latitudes of the Northern Hemisphere, over the latter half of the twentieth century, it is likely that there has been a 2–4 per cent increase in the frequency of heavy precipitation events'. In other words, episodes of very heavy rain would seem to have become more prevalent in recent decades, and we can reasonably assume that this suspected trend has continued into the present century.

A further catalyst for flooding incidents may be the effect on growing plants of the increasing amounts of carbon dioxide in the Earth's atmosphere. In response to higher atmospheric concentrations of CO_2, plants constrict their *stomata*—the tiny pores they have on the surfaces of their leaves through which carbon dioxide is absorbed. The constriction in turn reduces the rate at which moisture can be exuded from the plants, and therefore leaves more water resident in the soil; this allows the ground to become more easily saturated, and ultimately, more prone to flooding in very wet conditions.

Most importantly, however, there seems little doubt that well-meant engineering works over past decades have also contributed significantly to the frequency of crises of this kind. Throughout the catchment of the Danube, large areas of wetlands have been drained, meanders have been straightened out, and high banks have been constructed on either side to cut off large segments of the river from its natural flood plain. The objective has been to protect adjacent lands from regular flooding by conveying the water downstream as quickly as possible to the Black Sea; the result, however, has been to create the conditions for periodic and comparatively sudden catastrophic surges of water down the river—water which in the more distant past might have been delayed for days or even weeks as it sloshed to and fro in a much more leisurely way across the Danube's natural flood plain.

WHEN TIMES WERE OUT OF JOINT

22 April 2006 ∼

Of all the wonders that I yet have heard,
It seem to me most strange that men should fear;
Seeing that death, a necessary end,
Will come when it will come.

Death came to William Shakespeare himself 390 years ago tomorrow, on 23 April 1616. Moreover, he is commonly said to have died on the same day as his Spanish counterpart, Miguel de Cervantes, who indeed also passed away on 23 April 1616. And yet, Cervantes died ten days earlier than Shakespeare. How can this be?

The confusion can be traced to Pope Gregory XIII's reform of the Julian Calendar, which by the time Gregory came to St Peter's throne in 1572 was seriously out of joint. The Papal bull *Inter gravissimas* issued in February 1582 decreed, *inter alia*, that the day following the feast of St Francis that year—5 October 1582—was to become 15 October. In this way, ten superfluous days were eliminated.

The Pope, of course, was head of the Catholic Church, so in Catholic countries throughout Europe, including Spain, the new calendar was adopted, if not on the appointed day, at least within a decent interval. In Protestant countries like Shakespeare's England, however, it became almost a matter of principle to resist the proposal, no matter how sensible the changes it implied might seem. And where the change did take place, it was not without significant disgruntlement.

The new calendar annoyed the peasantry, for example, since their traditional calendar lore, expressed in weather proverbs associated with the feastdays of particular saints, was greatly upset by the ten-day shift in time. The result, it was said, was

> *That we can now no longer know,*
> *When we should plough and delve and sow.*

Some were fearful, too, that the saints would be upset, and would not grant their accustomed favours if prayed to on the wrong day, while others argued that the new calendar was contrary to nature, and that even the birds were confused about when to sing and when to fly away.

Even the intelligentsia could demur. In 1588 the French writer Montaigne declared: 'The late ten days diminution of the Pope have taken me so low, that I cannot well recover myself. I grit my teeth but my mind is always ten days ahead or ten days behind. My neighbours still find their seasons of sowing and reaping, and the opportunity of doing their business with the hurtful and propitious days, just at the same time where they had always assigned them. So great an uncertainty there is throughout; so gross, obscure and dull is our understanding.'

It was not until long after Shakespeare's time, in 1752, that Britain changed to the so-called New Style calendar, and by then it was necessary to lose eleven days to bring the dates back into proper line.

WHEN ICE CLINGS TO THE STARBOARD BOW

25 *April* 2006 ∾

Ice is probably the most *noire* of the various *bêtes* that haunt an airline pilot in his daily work. When it adheres to the exterior surfaces of an aircraft, it affects performance in two ways. Firstly, like water, ice is a very heavy substance, and if it builds up on the wings in any quantity the extra weight may make it difficult for the aircraft to maintain its height. And secondly, the wings and other external surfaces of a modern aircraft have a shape very carefully designed to allow them to do their job effectively—to keep the aircraft in the air and make it easy to control; ice alters their shape, and thereby affects their aerodynamic characteristics.

Temperature decreases in the vertical at a rate of 2 or 3°C for every 1,000 feet, so even on the warmest of sunny days an aircraft does not have to climb very high to reach the so-called 'freezing level'. Once there, the most dangerous form of icing occurs when the aeroplane, flying through cloud, comes into contact with 'supercooled' water droplets—drops of water, either of the cloud itself or of rain, which are still in the liquid state even though the surrounding temperature may be well below zero; they spread out over the wings on impact and freeze immediately to form a layer of ice.

Modern aircraft have efficient ways of ridding themselves of this unwelcome accretion. Sometimes the leading edges of wing and tail surfaces have rubber skins which normally assume the contour of the aircraft; during icy conditions, however, these may be caused to pulsate by means of compressed air, thereby mechanically fragmenting and dislodging the offending ice.

Alternatively, a liquid with a very low freezing point is sprayed on the vulnerable parts of the airframe; it not only clears any ice already on the aircraft, but also provides a protective film to prevent a further build-up. And thirdly, heat, provided either electrically or in the form of hot air generated by the engines and directed through pipes to vulnerable surfaces, may be used for ice removal or prevention.

Ice accretion is not a major problem for jet aircraft, since they spend most of their flying lives in the high atmosphere where temperatures are very low indeed and where such clouds as they may encounter are composed of ice crystals rather than water droplets; ice crystals do not stick easily to an aircraft's surfaces, and jet engines, moreover, generate plenty of heat and power that can be diverted to de-icers. But icing is a very real issue for a light aircraft flying through a frontal system, and also for short-haul turboprop aircraft which operate at much lower altitudes than their jet-powered counterparts, and which, having less power, are more vulnerable to the drag caused by even the thinnest layer of ice.

A NIGHTMARE JOURNEY ON A PEACEFUL OCEAN

27 April 2006 ∾

Ferdinand Magellan perished in a minor skirmish 485 years ago today, on 27 April 1521. It happened on the small island of Mactan in what we now know as the Philippines, and death deprived him of the achievement, but not the honour, of being the first man to sail around the world. It was his lieutenant, Juan Sebastian del Cano, who completed the circumnavigation in the last remaining ship of an original five, and who received from Emperor Charles v a globe with the inscription *Primus Circumdedisti Me*: 'You were the first to go around me.' Del Cano had given practical proof that the Earth was round—but it is Magellan we remember.

Fernando de Magallanes was born in Lisbon of noble parents in 1480 but in his early thirties, feeling that his military prowess was not appreciated in his native Portugal, he put his services at the disposal of the Spanish king and future Holy Roman Emperor. Being a man of imagination and intelligence, Charles agreed to underwrite an attempt by Magellan to find a southwestern route to the East Indian Spice Islands, the Moluccas.

The fleet of five ships sailed from Seville on 20 September 1519. Magellan crossed the Atlantic, headed down the coast of South America, and in November 1520, having discovered at the southern tip of the continent the strait which now bears his name, he and three of his ships encountered the 'Sea of the South' which they then set out to cross.

It was a most appalling journey. The fleet first headed north along the Chilean coast, and then took a course northwestwards, but as provisions dwindled, Magellan and his crew were tortured by thirst, stricken by scurvy and reduced to eating grilled rats and worm-infested biscuits for their sustenance. Finally, on 6 March 1521, the voyagers made landfall on the island of Guam, where they obtained fresh food for the first time in 99 days. But there had been one bright spot in the whole ordeal: the weather remained miraculously fair throughout, producing not a single storm for almost four months, and because of this singular indulgence Magellan and his men called this new ocean 'the Pacific'.

Of course, they had been lucky; the Pacific has its stormy interludes like any other ocean. On the other hand, it is indeed a more peaceful place than, for example, the Atlantic. The Pacific trade winds are generally weaker and less persistent, and the intervening belt of equatorial calm is wider, than their Atlantic counterparts. Moreover, partly on account of the ocean's great extent, and partly because there exists no wide opening to the Arctic regions, the general flow of the atmosphere from west to east is less disturbed in the North Pacific than in the North Atlantic, a circumstance that reflects itself in less volatility of the elements in the middle latitudes.

A SLIGHTLY DEVIOUS MONTH

1 *May* 2006 ∽

The month of May takes its generally genial nature from the fact that at this time of year cyclonic activity in the Atlantic is at its weakest. Depressions tend to be small and few, and very often linger in the vicinity of Newfoundland rather than sweep across the Atlantic to wreak havoc on our Irish shores. At this time of year, too, their average track takes them north of Ireland, so we escape the worst of their effects.

But they say, too, that you cannot trust this month. Now and then, as Shakespeare says, 'Rough winds do shake the darling buds of May', and we all know of the traditional advice that:

> *The wind at North and East*
> *Was never good for man or beast;*
> *So never think to cast a clout*
> *Until the month of May be out.*

And the poet James Russell Lowell is even more accusatorial, alleging that:

> *May is a pious fraud of the almanac,*
> *A ghastly parody of real Spring,*
> *Shaped out of snow, and breathed with eastern wind.*

In Ireland, however, by the time May arrives the probability of snow has become very small—albeit not quite zero; on average a fall of snow occurs once every five to ten years, although even if it does come, it is usually pretty harmless, amounting to little more than a flake or two. Moreover, despite the old 'nut-gathering' nursery rhyme, cold and frosty mornings are few and far between; there are only five of them in an average May. But Irish tradition has it that the early days of May often contain a short snap of unseasonably cold weather, a phenomenon regular enough to have been given a name: *Scairbhín na gCuac.*

But by and large, this is a gentle, unobtrusive month, not given to extremes, and with spring approaching its maturity, May provides welcome hints of the warmth of an approaching summer. The temperature on a typical May afternoon can be expected to reach 14 to 16°C, a degree or two higher than the usual for April. Once or twice during the month, the temperature may creep above 200C, and indeed in the last few days of May in 1922 the thermometer touched the record value of 28°C at a number of places.

An average day in May has about six hours of sunshine. We are also at that time of year when as a general rule there is comparatively little rainfall; April, May and June are the driest months in Ireland, with low-lying parts of the country normally experiencing less than 75 mm of precipitation.

Indeed, in general this is a bright, mellow month, a time of optimism when it seems winter can be finally declared over. 'Hard is the heart', says Chaucer, 'that loveth nought in May.'

WISE WORDS FROM CUCKOO-LAND

2 May 2006 ～

Gervase Markham was a writer of prose and poetry of considerable talent who lived about 400 years ago. Indeed, he was so good at it that he is a member of that select band who are sometimes suspected of having written some or all of William Shakespeare's plays. But here is another thing not a lot of people know: this same Gervase Markham, apparently, was the inspiration for the swaggering and grandiloquent character of Don Adriano de Armado in *Love's Labour Lost*. It is the latter, you may recall, who at the end of that long last scene of what, to keep things simple, we will continue to call Shakespeare's play, introduces the famous 'owl and cuckoo' song, which starts like this:

> *When daisies pied and violets blue*
> *And lady-smocks all silver-white,*
> *And cuckoo-buds of yellow hue*
> *Do paint the meadows with delight,*
> *The cuckoo then, on every tree,*
> *Mocks married men; for thus sings he: Cuckoo;*
> *Cuckoo, cuckoo—O word of fear,*
> *Unpleasing to a married ear!*

The association between adultery and the cuckoo, and hence the word 'cuckold', arises from the cuckoo's distinguishing characteristic of depositing its eggs in the nests of other birds. And it is around now that this kind of thing is liable to happen. Apparently the average date of the first cuckoo-call in the extreme southeast of England is around 1 April, while that in Norfolk, some distance to the north, is 25 April; here in Ireland, too, the bias seems to be towards the second half of April.

One's activity when the distinctive cry is heard for the first time may have a profound impact on one's well-being for the remainder of the year. It is considered lucky, for example, to be out walking when the cuckoo is first heard. If, on the other hand, you hear it from your bed, someone near and dear to you will fall ill before the cuckoo goes. Moreover, if you have no money in your pocket when it calls, or if you do not carefully turn over every coin upon your person, you are destined to be poor for the remainder of the year.

The cuckoo's song is also a timely reminder to look around to see if nature locally is up to schedule. *'Nuair a sheinneas an chuach ar chrann gan duilleóg, díol do bhó is cheannaigh arán'*, the saying goes. The theory is that if the budding of the trees is not well advanced before the cuckoo comes, the growing season is retarded and you may not have sufficient grass to feed your cow; you should dispose of it, and stock up with bread and other foods instead. The English version expresses much the same idea:

> *When the cuckoo comes to an empty thorn.*
> *Sell your horse and buy some corn.*

THE GREATLY EXAGGERATED DEATH OF SHERLOCK HOLMES

4 May 2006 ∽

It was indeed a fearsome place. The torrent, swollen by the melting snow, plunges into a tremendous abyss, from which the spray rolls up like smoke from a burning house. The shaft into which the river hurls itself is an immense chasm, lined by glistening, coal-black rock, and narrowing into a creaming, boiling pit of incalculable depth. The long sweep of green water roaring forever down, and the thick flickering curtain of spray hissing forever upwards, turn a man giddy with their constant whirl.

Thus went Dr Watson's description of the forbidding Reichenbach Falls in the Bernese Oberland, over which Sherlock Holmes and his arch-enemy, Professor Moriarty, tumbled to their deaths 115 years ago today. That, at least, was the inference intended by Arthur Conan Doyle when he first recounted, in *The Final Problem*, the events of 4 May 1891.

The tragedy marked the putative end of a brilliant sleuthing career in which the weather, and particularly rain, had often played a major part. Towards the end of his very first adventure, *A Study in Scarlet*, for example, Holmes tells Watson: 'The very first thing which I observed on arriving there was that a cab had made two ruts with its wheels close to the curb. Now, up to last night, we have had no rain for a week, so that those wheels which left such a deep impression must have been there during the night. Since the cab was there after the rain began, and was not there at any time during the morning, it follows that it must have been there during the night.' These facts, combined with two convenient sets of footprints, permit the detective a gigantic intellectual leap to the clear conclusion that the cabby 'done it'.

In *The Boscombe Valley Mystery*, on the other hand, the solution was 'entirely a matter of barometric pressure'. It turns out that Holmes had noticed before he left home that the glass was high. Provided it remained so, rain was unlikely to occur before he got a chance to search for clues at the scene of the crime. A sudden downpour, on the other hand, would have washed away all the footprints that Holmes needed to solve his case.

And rain is again crucial in *The Musgrave Ritual*. The lack of footprints in the vicinity, despite rain the previous evening, allows Holmes to deduce that the butler had never left the house; in this case he clearly saw that the butler did not do it.

But all this meteorological ingenuity ended abruptly at the Reichenbach Falls—or did it? As it happened, Holmes reappeared in London three years later by popular demand. It turned out that only Moriarty, and not Holmes, had died that day on the falls at Reichenbach; the great detective resumed his cerebral career with *The Empty House*.

HOW WET DOES THE OCEAN GET?

5 *May* 2006 ～

Measuring rainfall over land is simple, and the methodology has changed little in two thousand years. All you need is a container to collect the water; if you know the area of the mouth of the container, a little mathematics allows you to calculate 'the depth to which a flat and impermeable surface would be covered by water in a given period, assuming that none of the liquid disappears by run-off or evaporation'.

But it is much more difficult to gather rainfall data out at sea, since, apart from anything else, there is rarely anyone there to measure it. You can ask friendly ships' officers to take rainfall readings, but two significant problems immediately arise: firstly, the heaving and rolling of the ship, and the turbulence generated in the local airflow by its superstructure, seriously diminish the representative nature of any samples collected by a rain gauge; and secondly, ships do their best to avoid areas of turbulent weather altogether, and these, unfortunately, are the places rain falls most abundantly.

Modern technology, however, has produced ingenious possibilities. Most depend on instruments mounted on moored or drifting buoys, which being relatively small, cause little distortion of the local airflow. The simplest way is to measure electronically at regular intervals the depth of water in a container, and have the readings transmitted back to base by satellite; when full, the container empties itself automatically by some siphoning arrangement. An alternative is to monitor electronically the way in which falling raindrops attenuate the signal between a light source and a receiver. And a third method involves measuring the momentum of each falling raindrop as it strikes a pressure-sensitive plate, and transforming the multitude of such signals into a quantity of rain per given period.

But perhaps the cleverest of all is an acoustic method. We have all from time to time inferred an intuitive idea of the heaviness of rain from the sound it makes when falling on a roof above our heads. This concept can be exploited with a hydrophone—an underwater microphone; located some distance below the surface, the hydrophone records the sound of the rain impacting on the water, and from this a computer calculates the likely rate of rainfall.

Weather radar, as used on land to measure rainfall, can be employed in the same way at sea when mounted on a ship; but data for a given area depend on a suitably, and very expensively, equipped vessel happening to be in the vicinity at the time. Increasingly nowadays, satellites are used to estimate rainfall; infra-red sensors on the spacecraft measure the temperatures of cloud-tops on the image, from which their approximate height can be deduced, which may in turn be loosely converted into the likely amount of rain falling beneath them. As a method of measuring rainfall, it seems crude—but it is surprisingly effective.

A VERY SPECIAL KIND OF BOX

8 *May* 2006 ∽

Boxes of various standard kinds were a notable feature of life when I was growing up. Oranges, for example, came in orange boxes which were about three feet long, one foot square in cross-section, and were constructed of a flimsy wood with metal strapping; for some reason that I never knew, they were divided into two compartments. Butter boxes, on the other hand, were much sturdier and, for some equally unknown reason, they tapered towards the base; they were about 18 inches square at the top, but only about a foot square at the bottom—very strange, since as far as I know they were intended to contain rectangular pounds of butter.

Another familiar container was the plywood tea chest, about two foot cubed and invaluable for moving house, while biscuit boxes were of tin, cubes again with sides some 18 inches long. There were many more, all of which served for different kinds of storage, or even as cheap and useful furniture, when no longer needed for their original intended function.

Long gone are all these different boxes, but meteorologists have a type of box which has survived for 140 years. It is made of wood, or sometimes nowadays of plastic; it is typically about three feet wide, eighteen inches tall and one foot deep, and it has louvred sides invariably painted white. It is called a Stevenson screen.

The screen, one of the classic designs of all time, was designed by Thomas Stevenson, father of the author Robert Louis, and its function is to house thermometers. It rests on a metal stand whose height ensures that the bulbs of the thermometers inside are exactly four feet above the ground; it is made of wood or plastic because these materials absorb heat slowly and are therefore not directly affected by radiant heat from the Sun; it is white for the same reason—to reflect the sunlight rather than absorb its heat; and the louvred sides allow air to circulate freely inside the chamber, while the thermometers are shielded from the direct effects of wind and rain.

Inside, two thermometers are mounted vertically side by side: the 'dry bulb' thermometer gives the air temperature in the normal way, while the 'wet-bulb' has its bulb enclosed in a damp 'sock' of white muslin, kept moist by a cotton wick immersed in distilled water. The wet-bulb thermometer gives a lower reading than its dry counterpart, and the difference between the two values is a measure of the relative humidity. Usually there are two additional thermometers, specially designed to indicate respectively the highest and lowest temperatures experienced since they were last re-set.

The whole ensemble is orientated with the louvred door of the screen facing north, thereby avoiding any danger of the

thermometers being subjected to direct sunlight, even moment-
arily, while being read by an observer.

THE DELUGES AND
DROUGHTS OF CHERRAPUNJI

9 *May* 2006 ∿

During the British Raj in India, officials posted to the
extreme northeast had a life expectancy of only a few
years. Even today by all accounts, the local inhabitants of
the hostile, bleak and treeless southern slopes of the Khasi Hills
are unusually fatalistic and submissive, almost as if their human
instinct for survival had been undermined. Little wonder, some
might say; this part of India is paradoxically a virtual desert and
also one of the wettest places in the world.

The town of Cherrapunji in this region has an average annual
rainfall of 11,430 millimetres, more than ten times that of Ireland.
Between August 1860 and July 1861 it experienced 26,000 mm of
rain, the most recorded anywhere in a 12-month period, and
the 9,300 mm measured in July 1861 is still a global record for a
calendar month. More recently, the town accumulated yet another
record.

Until three years ago, the most rainfall ever experienced in a
day in Cherrapunji was the 1,036 mm recorded on 14 June 1876.
The world record, an impressive 1,840 mm, was held by the
quaintly named district of Foc-Foc on the island of La Reunion,
east of Madagascar in the Indian Ocean. But then on 10 June 2003,

Cherrapunji had 1,840 mm, and added yet another global record to its list.

The heavy rains at Cherrapunji are a consequence of the summer monsoon which sets in each year in late May or early June. With the coming of spring, the hot Sun moving northwards causes the air over southern Asia to expand and become lighter, and low pressure develops over the region. Then warm, moist air from the ocean, moving anticlockwise around this low, streams in over India from the Arabian Sea, and as it is forced to rise over the terrain that slopes gently upwards towards the Himalayas, its moisture condenses, bringing torrential rain to the entire subcontinent.

The average rainfall rises roughly with the altitude, but the zone of maximum precipitation occurs, not at the summits of the Himalayas, but in a relatively narrow strip of varying altitude on their windward side. Cherrapunji, at an altitude of 1,313 metres, is exactly in this zone, and for six months of the year, from April to September, the heavy rain is almost incessant.

Over the centuries, the summer rains have washed away the topsoil in the region, so there is nothing to retain the water. Most of it cascades down to irrigate the rice fields on the plains of Bangladesh, or sinks irrecoverably into the porous limestone subsoil of the area. Then in October, the monsoon winds reverse direction; no rain falls until the following spring, and the arid ground is baked lifeless by sun and desiccating winds. The recently drenched inhabitants of Cherrapunji suffer severe drought, and go about such business as they have at a weary, listless pace.

THE FORMATION OF FAIR-WEATHER FOG

10 *May* 2006 ∽

*C*eo *soininne ar aibhnibh, ceo doininne ar chnocaibh,* goes the old saying: the fog that forms in river valleys is a fair-weather fog, while that on hills is associated with poor weather. The latter, of course, is simply low cloud—cloud low enough to brush the hilltops during periods of actual or threatened rain. But for real fog to form, a delicate balance is required between the various weather elements.

Air always contains a modicum of moisture in the form of water vapour. The amount of moisture it can comfortably accommodate, however, is crucially dependent on its temperature: the colder the air, the less moisture it can hold, and *vice versa.* If the temperature of a volume of air falls sufficiently, sooner or later it will reach a point where it must rid itself of some moisture, and the excess condenses into tiny drops of water. The result is dew, hoar frost, cloud or fog, depending on the circumstances.

The *ceo soininne* most commonly occurs near the centre of an anticyclone, when winds are light and the daytime conditions relatively good. It depends for its existence on the fact that during clear, starry nights any solar heat absorbed by our planet during the day is re-radiated into space. The air itself is more or less immune from such radiation; it takes its temperature from the surface with which it is in contact, so it is the gradual cooling of the ground on clear nights that provides the initial stimulus for fog. On a cloudy night, by contrast, the cloud acts like a blanket over the Earth to prevent any dramatic fall in temperature.

The strength of the wind, however, is crucial to what happens next. In the simplest case, with no wind at all, only air in immediate contact with the ground is cooled to the point of condensation, and the exuded moisture takes the form of dew—or a white crystalline hoar frost if the temperature is low enough. If, on the other hand, there is a strong breeze, the resulting turbulence continually replaces air cooled by contact with the ground with warmer air from higher up; the loss of heat is spread over a considerable depth of atmosphere, and the chances are that nowhere will the temperature fall low enough for condensation to occur.

The intermediate case, however—a slight but noticeable movement of the air—results in fog. The slight turbulence in these circumstances allows cooling to be spread through a layer of air anything from, say, three to 30 metres in depth, a layer that is sufficiently shallow for the temperature of the entire volume of air within it to be lowered to the point where condensation into droplets must take place. After a short while the landscape is totally obscured.

THE MAN WHO MOVED THE CONTINENTS

12 *May* 2006 ∼

Alfred Lothar Wegener was a German meteorologist who, early in the twentieth century, contributed very significantly to our knowledge of the thermal structure of the upper atmosphere. But it is not for this he is remembered. In fact, during the later part of his life and for some years afterwards he was regarded as something of a crank; he had this zany notion that the continents had been wandering around the surface of the Earth for millions and millions of years.

The concept of *continental drift* was not entirely original to Wegener. As long ago as 1620 the English philosopher and chancellor to James I, Francis Bacon, had looked at a map of the world and noted that Africa and South America appeared capable of fitting together like two adjacent pieces of a jigsaw puzzle. But Wegener developed the drift theory, drawing widely on paleoclimatic evidence; he proposed it first in 1912, and enlarged on his ideas in *The Origins of Continents and Oceans*, published in 1915.

Two hundred million years ago, Wegener maintained, the Earth had only one great land mass, which he called *Pangea*—'all lands'. Then about 180 million years ago it split into two parts, which drifted slowly away from each other. To the north was what subsequently came to be called *Laurasia*—North America, Europe and Asia, still joined together. *Gondwanaland*, comprising South America, Africa, India and Australia, lay to the south. One hundred and thirty-five million years ago South America began to break away from Africa, and the South Atlantic Ocean filled the gap between.

Wegener visualised the continents as large rafts of granite, ploughing in slow motion through a great basaltic sea and throwing up mountains like bow waves on their leading edges. It was a bizarre and courageous theory, and was loudly rejected, not without ridicule, by the scientific establishment during Wegener's lifetime.

Despite his peers' scepticism on this particular issue, Wegener was recognised as a world expert on polar meteorology and glaciology. He undertook several expeditions to Greenland, and indeed it was there in early 1931, shortly after his fiftieth birthday, that he and a companion became lost upon the icecap. Several months later a search party came upon a pair of skis stuck upright in the snow, with a broken ski-pole lying in between; seventy-five years ago today, on 12 May 1931, lying in the ice beneath, they found the body of a man, 'his face calm and peaceful, almost smiling'. It was Alfred Wegener.

Not until the late 1950s did better geological mapping and new techniques for magnetic observations make it clear that Wegener had been right, and that at one time the continents had indeed been joined together. Wegener's theories entered mainstream geophysics, and became the basis of the modern science of *plate tectonics.*

ON STRIPS AND STRIPES

13 *May* 2006 ∽

Between the end of the RTÉ news at six-o-one and the weather forecast about five to seven, one is invariably obliged to endure several interludes of soccer. You will notice, if you stay awake, that the patch of grass on which these Spurs and Gunners, Hammers, Magpies and Canaries run purposefully up and down and hug each other when they get excited, is tastefully arrayed with stripes and other pretty patterns brought about by someone having mown it in a certain way.

But why? The blades of grass, which collectively make up the playing pitch are, by and large, identical. And blades of grass are green—not forty shades of it, or even two. Just green!

The answer lies in how grass reacts to light that falls on it. Almost any object, be it a blade of grass or anything else, appears to be a certain colour because its molecular structure is such as to absorb certain wavelengths of light and to reflect others. In the case of grass, all colours except those that make up the colour green are absorbed; the unabsorbed green light is 'rejected' and registers as that colour when it hits our eyes.

When sunlight hits a blade of grass at an oblique angle, however, some of the incident light in *all* parts of the spectrum is reflected before the process of selective absorption can take place. This, for an observer, has the effect of overlaying the green with a whitish tinge, its extent depending on the angle; the green therefore appears lighter or darker than it would if the leaf were viewed from some different perspective.

Now mowing a football pitch, particularly when the cutting blades are followed by a roller, causes nearly all the blades of grass mown in the one direction to acquire a common orientation; when the mower turns and cuts a parallel stripe the opposite way, this second set of leaves acquires a different, but again nearly uniform, orientation. The sunlight therefore hits the blades of grass in two adjacent strips at a different angle, so they reflect and absorb the incident light in differing proportions, and give a different perception to the eye.

Once the Spurs and Hammers start their game, of course, this careful orientation of the blades of grass is totally disturbed, and the patterns quickly disappear. Moreover, if you rarely see the same effect on the patch of grass you call a lawn *chez vous*, it is probably because you mow the grass in a somewhat random way, and do not go up and down, and up and down, with care. Try it, and you will achieve the desired effect—and if you view the stripes from one end of your lawn, and then move to observe them from the other, you will find the shading on the alternating stripes reversed.

THE INTERPRETATION OF VOLCANIC RUMBLINGS

15 *May* 2006 ～

Meteorologically, the island of Java in Indonesia is famous for being the most thundery location on the planet, as reckoned by the average number of days per year on which thunderstorms occur. At any one spot on that island you are likely to hear thunder on 223 days out of the 365. But, as we have been reminded in recent days by the rumblings of Mount Merapi, Java is also said to have the highest density of volcanoes in the world.

Volcanoes do not occur just anywhere on the Earth's surface, although at some time in the past everywhere on the Earth's surface has experienced them. The most vulnerable spots are located along the joints between the vast tectonic plates that make up the Earth's crust, and more than two-thirds of all eruptions take place around the rim of the Pacific Ocean, with such a frequency that vulcanologists have dubbed this zone 'the ring of fire'. And the ring's most active region is in the vicinity of Java.

In biblical times, volcanic eruptions were looked upon as instruments of the Almighty, to be used as required for disciplinary purposes, but today's scientists like to be able to anticipate such vengeful whims. One of the more obvious signs of a major event is the development of minor volcanic activity where there was none before. But it is often difficult to tell in this case if a volcano is merely 'clearing its throat', as it were, or building up for catastrophe. More subtle methods are needed to obtain a clearer picture.

One common technique is to observe closely the physical shape of the volcanic mountain. The subterranean movement of the magma often causes a volcano to 'swell' slightly, so a subtle change in shape may be the precursor of a major event. Other clues can be deduced from seismic activity in the vicinity; the rising magma results in seismic groanings and creakings deep beneath the Earth's surface, and the final warning of a major eruption is often a chorus of rumblings more insistent than any heard before—a seismic drum-roll known as a 'volcanic tremor'. And a third methodology involves the use of infra-red radiometers on satellites to detect threatening hot-spots in the vicinity of a volcano.

By combining these techniques, vulcanologists now achieve regular success in predicting *when* and *where* volcanic eruptions will occur—unlike those who try to predict earthquakes, a discipline in which accurate forecasts are elusive. But vulcanologists have still not mastered the art of predicting *how big* an eruption to expect—whether it will be a relatively minor event and do no great harm to anyone, or result in a cataclysmic explosion on the scale of Pinatubo in the Philippines back in 1991. This is the penultimate challenge of the science; the last will be to prevent eruptions altogether.

THE BUBBLES IN THE VICAR'S POND

16 *May* 2006 ～

The eighteenth-century cleric John Pointer was a distinguished fellow of Merton College, Oxford, an antiquary of some renown and, in his spare time, vicar of Slapton in Northamptonshire. And he also had an interest in the weather.

His *magnum opus* on this topic was a light-hearted pamphlet published in 1723 with the resounding title *A Rational Account of The Weather, Shewing the Signs of its Several Changes and Alterations, together with the Philosophical Reasons of Them.*

Pointer had little time for scientific attempts at weather prediction, particularly those involving barometers or other instruments, but instead urged his readers to put their faith in natural signs. He was impressed, for example, by the prognostic capabilities of the Slapton village pond: 'When rain approaches it becomes troubled, rising full of bubbles and in a little time thickening with a yellow scum, which presently, as it rains, washes away. The worthy Mr Fowler, an inhabitant of this place, has freely confessed that he has often been admonished by it in time of harvest to bring in his corn.'

Now, Rev. Pointer's notion is not as daft as you might think. To understand why, cast your mind back to the little knick-knacks found in Christmas crackers. Among them, sometimes, will be a little plastic figure of a deep-sea diver; when you put it in a bottle filled with water and replace the cork, it is possible to make the figure rise to the top or sink into the depths by a slight manipulation of the cork.

The device is called a 'Cartesian diver', and its working principle, allegedly discovered by the French philosopher René Descartes, is very simple. The figure's helmet has a cavity, in which a bubble of air is trapped when the diver is immersed. If the diver is floating near the surface of the water, supported by the bubble's buoyancy, then pushing downwards on the cork increases pressure everywhere inside the bottle; this causes compression of the air that forms the bubble, and the volume of the bubble is decreased. Since the diver's buoyancy, by the principle of Archimedes, depends on the combined volume of the diver and his bubble, the shrinking of the bubble ultimately overcomes the diver's tendency to float—and he sinks to the bottom of the bottle. To make him rise again, it is only necessary to adjust the cork so that pressure is reduced, the bubble expands, and the diver shoots to the surface.

Now the theory goes that 'effervescence of decay' produces bubbles at the bottom of a village pond that cling to particles of mud. Rain is often preceded by a fall in atmospheric pressure; as the pressure drops, the bubbles in the pond increase in size, become more buoyant, and shoot to the surface, bringing with them thousands of tiny specks of adhering mud—to cause a scum.

MAY IS NOT PLAYING BY THE RULES

18 *May* 2006 ∼

Best known of all the Byngs, undoubtedly, is the Admiral John, who in 1757, having done less than might have been expected of him to defend the island of Minorca from the French, was executed by firing squad in Portsmouth Harbour on his own flagship. His fate prompted the French author Voltaire to remark in *Candide* that the English found it necessary from time to time to shoot an admiral *pour encourager les autres*—'in order to encourage the others'.

Meteorologically, however, the Admiral's namesake and nephew, John Byng, 5th Viscount Torrington, is of much more significance. It was the latter who remarked in 1797: 'Surely summers were different formerly; or is it youth, the season of sunshine? For then

I thought the summers bright and warm; but now in my age they appear cold and cheerless.' It is a theme echoed by Yeats in 'The Meditation of the Old Fisherman':

> *In the Junes that were warmer than these are,*
> *the waves were more gay,*
> *When I was a boy with never a crack in my heart.*

The same, as we have seen in recent days, can happen to the month of May. May was never like this when I was young. May ought to be, and nearly always is, a shy, retiring, gentle month, providing welcome hints of the warmth of an approaching summer. At this time of year, cyclonic activity in the Atlantic ought to be at its very weakest; the depressions should be few and rather small; and their average track should take them well to the north of Ireland, allowing us to escape the worst of their effects.

But depressions do not read the textbooks, and each that comes along is unique in its own peculiar way. Many obey the rules prescribed in the preceding paragraph, but now and then a few come farther south, others head north, and the odd maverick may venture where no depression has ever dared to go before.

Lows are also idiosyncratic in their volatility. The classic example begins as a very small feature off the eastern seaboard of the United States, develops into a full-blooded depression over the ocean well to the west of Ireland, and then begins to decay in the vicinity of Norway; others, like those we have seen in recent days, move farther south and conserve their worst fury until adjacent to our shores. The family of depressions which caused our recent rains and gales came very close to Ireland, and in some cases passed right across the island. Generally speaking, the closer a depression comes, the heavier will be its rain, and stronger the associated gales.

But then, if depressions all followed the same path, or if there were a means of ascertaining beyond doubt the track that any individual might follow, the forecaster's lot would be a very dull and dreary one indeed.

QUINCENTENARY OF A CONQUISTADOR

20 *May* 2006 ∿

In 1479, while visiting his brother-in-law who was Governor of Porto Santo in Madeira, Christopher Columbus noted that the island was situated in a zone of steady northeasterly winds. He is said to have put this observation to good use more than a decade later when planning his famous 'enterprise of the Indies', by plotting a very southerly course to take advantage of the trades.

Columbus, in fact, enjoyed ideal conditions on this voyage. There were no storms, hurricanes or debilitating calms, and he made such rapid progress westwards that he was obliged to keep two reckonings of the distance covered. One of these he kept to himself; the other he announced to the crew—a deliberate under-estimate to avoid their panic at having ventured so far into the unknown.

But in due course even the good weather became a source of anxiety for the crew. The weather was fine—but would it ever rain again, or would they die of thirst? The winds were steady—but would they ever find winds to blow them home again, or would the wind always blow from the east in these uncharted seas? But finally, on 12 October 1492, thirty-six days after leaving the Canaries, Columbus set foot on what he called Guanahani, believed to be the island that we now know as San Salvador.

The home voyage, too, began propitiously. On the mistaken assumption that the way back to Spain lay due northeast, Columbus headed farther north than strictly necessary—and fortuitously found the fastest route to Europe in the prevailing westerlies. Only as his two ships approached the Azores did a succession of fierce storms impede their progress, those from 12 to 17 February, and from 26 February to 4 March 1493, being graphically described by Columbus in his writings. 'It is very painful', he wrote in the case of the latter storm, 'to have such a tempest when we are already at the doors of home.' But next morning, his ships were in the shelter of the river Tagus; although he had found land in rival Portugal, and not Spain as might have been preferred, at least Columbus was on the right side of the Atlantic.

This first 'encounter' with the New World, as it is euphemistically described in these days of political correctness, was the highpoint of Columbus's career. He made three more transatlantic voyages but proved to be an inept administrator, with little talent for political intrigue. Moreover, despite mounting evidence to the contrary, he was adamant for the remainder of his life that he had reached Cathay, or China, and his perversity in this respect diminished his credibility, hindering his ambitions of nobility and wealth. He died in Valladolid, aged fifty-four, a bitter and disillusioned man, 500 years ago today on 20 May 1506.

SPRING FEVER IN THE SUMMERTIME

25 *May* 2006 ∽

Hay-fever, in a way, is a relatively recent ailment. Two hundred years ago the medical world was unaware of its existence, until in 1819 a London doctor called John Bostock, himself a sufferer from what he described as 'an unusual train of symptoms', published an account of them. Once identified, the condition, which involved periodic bouts of itchy and watery eyes, a runny nose, and persistent sneezing, was observed to be a prevalent one and was known to the medical fraternity for many years as 'Bostock's catarrh'. Around mid-century it was discovered that the symptoms were an allergic reaction to tiny grains of pollen suspended in the atmosphere.

Pollen is a fine, powdery substance exuded for reproductive purposes by plants. Concentrations tend to be high outdoors from the middle of May to early August, reaching a maximum during June and early July. The worst culprits for producing spores are wind-pollinated plants like grass, ragweed and birch trees, which must release vast amounts of pollen in order to ensure that some will reach its target; insect-pollinated plants, on the other hand—those with colourful flowers or strong scents—produce far less. Since the pollen from the various grasses was the worst offender, the ailment came to be known as 'hay fever'.

The amount of pollen in the air at any given time depends on several meteorological factors. First of all, the extrusion of pollen by plants—a process known as *anthesis*—shows a variation throughout the day which is related to temperature and to light intensity. Secondly, the extent to which the pollen particles, once expelled by the plant, are collected by the air, depends on the wind strength at the time; in very calm conditions the pollen is shed slowly, and is less likely to become suspended in the air.

Another important factor is the degree of *instability* present in the atmosphere—the extent to which there is a tendency for vertical currents of air to develop. If there is a great deal of vertical motion, the pollen is dispersed throughout a deep layer of the atmosphere, thus reducing dramatically the count near ground level. But perhaps the greatest effect is caused by rain; a shower of rain 'washes' the air, and significantly reduces the pollen concentration. Heavy rain, of which we have experienced a great deal of late, may even disrupt the process of anthesis altogether.

The pollen content of the air is measured with a 'spore trap', which draws air through a narrow opening in such a way that the spores impact on a sticky microscopic slide. Forecasts of likely pollen levels are carried out by feeding all the relevant parameters, including meteorological predictions, into a computer programme which carries out computations based on known relationships between the variables. The result is a 'pollen count' prediction for the following day.

WHY WINDS BLOW HATS AWAY

26 *May* 2006 ∾

The annals of classical literature are silent as to which erudite and eminent Roman scribe composed the celebrated *Rune of the Old Man's Hat*. It has come down to us, however, as an eloquent exemplar of Muddle Latin, at once transcendent and bathetic in its empathy with the human condition in its constant struggle with the elements. Let me quote for you the opening lines:

> *Prope ripam fluvii solus,*
> *A senex silently sat;*
> *Super capitum ecce his wig,*
> *Et wig super, ecce his hat.*
> *Blew Zephrus alte, acerbus,*
> *Dum elderly gentleman sat;*
> *Et a capite took up quite torve,*
> *Et in rivum proiecit, his hat.*

The hat problem—and as you may guess, the subsequent influmenation of the wig—was due almost entirely to the gustiness of the wind. Wind occurs in the first place because of differences in atmospheric pressure over the Earth's surface, which bring about a movement of air from one place to another. But there is always some element of turbulence in this flow of air; even over a few seconds the wind increases and decreases in strength as periodic gusts are followed by short, temporary lulls. Three factors determine the extent of the turbulence: the roughness of the surface over which the air is passing; the speed of the wind itself; and the extent to which the flow of air is disturbed by eddies of rising air caused by solar heating.

Surface roughness affects the wind in much the same way as rocks on a riverbed disturb the flow of water. If the ground is relatively smooth, or if the air is passing over a calm sea, the flow will be relatively steady and undisturbed. But over an uneven surface eddies form, and are carried away by the wind, becoming apparent as gustiness downstream. The rougher the surface, the greater the tendency for turbulence; the effect is particularly noticeable when a strong wind passes over buildings, trees or rugged countryside.

The degree of turbulence is also affected by the speed of the wind. Any fluid will flow smoothly if its speed is sufficiently low, but above a certain limit the flow becomes unstable and breaks down into turbulent motion—like a river in flood. So when the wind increases above a certain strength, even over relatively smooth terrain, the airflow breaks down and becomes turbulent.

Thermal turbulence, finally, occurs when the smooth flow of the air is disturbed, not by the direct effects of the surface underneath, but by convective currents set up by solar heating of the ground. The horizontal motion of the wind, impeded in this way by rising currents, results in gustiness downstream. Indeed the most blustery and unpredictable winds occur in showery conditions, when powerful downdrafts in the vicinity of the shower clouds distort the flow of wind and often make it quite chaotic.

THE CLIMATIC AMBIENCE OF *MADAME BOVARY*

27 *May* 2006 ∽

Rouen is just far enough away from Cherbourg to make a welcome coffee stop. I have sat often in the sunshine in the small cathedral square, mesmerised less by the imposing edifice itself than by the ubiquitous sparrows who try so cheekily to share your croissants. Often, too, I have noted in the nearby Place des Carmes the statue of a baggy-trousered, moustachioed, nineteenth-century figure, one of Rouen's most famous sons, Gustave Flaubert, and resolved that I must read his masterpiece. And now I have just finished *Madame Bovary*.

Emma Bovary is one of the great anti-heroines of all time. She is the nineteenth-century 'desperate housewife', a young country doctor's wife whose life is meaningless and empty, and who has romantic dreams whose indulgence leads to her personal, social and financial ruin, and ultimately to suicide. *Madame Bovary* was sufficiently shocking in its time for Flaubert to be prosecuted, albeit unsuccessfully, for offending public morals, and the novel is as disturbingly relevant today as when first published in 1857.

It has its weather, too. The *mise en scène* is Yonville, a fictitious country town northeast of Rouen, and the book's most memorable protagonist, apart from Emma Bovary, is the self-serving, bombastic, semi-comical Homais, the local pharmacist. He provides the new doctor and his wife with what seems, at first, a plausible summary of the climatology of that part of Normandy.

'Actually, the climate is not bad,' the Bovarys are told, 'and we even include in the vicinity a few nonagenarians. The thermometer drops as low as four degrees in winter, and, in high summer, touches twenty-five, thirty centigrade at the very most, which gives us a maximum of twenty-four, or else fifty-four Fahrenheit, no more! We are sheltered from the north wind by the Forest of Argueil on one side, and from the west wind by the Côte Saint-Jean.'

But then the pharmacist's innate verbosity takes over, casting serious doubts on the entire spectrum of his scientific acumen: 'This heat, you see, which on account of the water vapour given off by the river and the considerable presence of cattle in the meadows, which exhale, as you know, a good deal of ammonia, that's to say nitrogen, hydrogen and oxygen, and which, sucking up the humus from the soil, mingling these several emanations, doing them up in a bundle, so to speak, and combining spontaneously with the electricity circulating in the atmosphere, whenever there is any, it could, as happens in the tropics, engender insalubrious miasmas.'

We find out later how Homais came to assume such a detailed knowledge of the local weather. He has made weather observations, and is the author of *Statistique generale du canton d'Yonville, suivie d'observations climatologiques*, or 'General Statistics of the Canton of Yonville, followed by Climatological Observations'. Happily, neither in fact nor fiction has this document survived.

AN ATMOSPHERIC TRIGGER FOR A TREMOR

29 *May* 2006 ∽

The conventional wisdom has it that earthquakes are entirely independent of the weather. Nonetheless, there has been a recurring suspicion down the centuries that atmospheric conditions may sometimes be a seismic catalyst—that changes in atmospheric pressure, for example, may sometimes trigger the beginning of a tremor.

Charles Darwin was one of the first to think about the matter seriously. In *The Voyage of the Beagle*, his account of the events leading to his theories on evolution, he writes: 'In northern Chile, the inhabitants are most firmly convinced of some connection between the state of the atmosphere and of the trembling of the ground. I was much struck by this, when mentioning to some people at Copiapo that there had been a sharp shock in a nearby town; they immediately cried, "How fortunate! There will be plenty of pasture there this year." And certainly, it did happen that on the very day of the earthquake a shower of rain fell.'

Darwin goes on to discount one contemporary view that the rain might be caused by vapours escaping from fissures in the ground, but gives qualified support to another theory: 'There appears much probability in the view that when the barometer is low, and when rain might naturally be expected to occur anyway, the diminished pressure of the atmosphere over a wide extent of country might well determine the precise day on which the earth, already stretched to the utmost by subterranean forces, should yield, crack, and consequently tremble.'

Then about ten years ago, a Japanese scientist called Masakazu Outake found evidence that appeared to link earthquakes to *high* pressure, rather than low. Looking back over centuries of records, he noticed that all 13 major Japanese earthquakes between AD684 and 1946 had occurred during the autumn and winter—a seasonal bias against whose happening by chance, it seems, the odds are something like 1,000 to one.

Outake also noted that the average monthly atmospheric pressure in the region is about 10 hectopascals higher between August and February than it is in the other half of the year: he believes that this may have something to do with the frequency of serious tremors in the winter months.

He points out that in the vicinity of Japan the Pacific plate is sliding like a wedge westwards and downwards beneath the Eurasian plate adjacent to it. The Japanese islands are situated on this latter, upper plate, and the extra 10 hectopascals of pressure on them during the winter months is the equivalent of 100 kg of weight on each square metre of territory; variations in the atmospheric pressure, moreover, affect the force exerted by the upper on the lower plate, and may at times, his theory goes, be sufficient to trigger a sudden relative movement of the two—in other words, an earthquake.

A LEGACY OF ANCIENT ROME

1 June 2006

'Time has no divisions to mark its passage,' wrote Thomas Mann in *The Magic Mountain.* 'There is never a thunderstorm or a blare of trumpets to announce the beginning of a new month or a new year—and even when a new century begins, it is only we mortals who ring bells and fire off pistols.'

Thus it was that at midnight last night we passed soundlessly from May to June. Both, like most of the calendar months we use today, are survivors from the Roman Empire. May is named after the goddess Maia, consort of Vulcan and daughter of Atlas who carried the whole world on his shoulders, while June is said to take its name from Juno, the very beautiful but jealous wife of Jupiter, chief god to the citizens of ancient Rome.

In the early days of Rome, its people observed a year comprising only ten months. They did not, as one might expect, divide the year decimally into ten approximately equal periods; not even the French Revolutionaries at their most fervent went that far. Instead the Romans recognised ten roughly lunar months from March to December, and then simply excluded from their nomenclature the 'dead' or 'fallow' period of the year—that which now comprises January and February. Although this may seem decidedly odd to us nowadays, it was—and apparently still is—a common practice among primitive peoples; parallels, it seems, have been found in places as far apart as Africa and New Zealand.

The early Roman calendar thus started with the month of March, called after Mars, the god of war. April, by contrast, was the gentle month which restored to Nature all its fruitfulness; *omnia aperit,* they used to say of it: 'It opens all things.' After May and June, however, the Roman imagination was exhausted; the other six months were simply 'Five' on up to 'Ten', or *Quintilis*, *Sextilis*, and the rest which are still with us as September, October, November and December. In a burst of grateful affection in 44BC, the Romans renamed Quintilis after Julius Caesar—our July—and some years later, in 8BC, the Emperor Augustus insisted on a similar honour, and gave his name to August.

Apparently it was the Etruscans, who lived in northern Italy in what we now know as Lombardy and Tuscany, who added January and February to bring the 'dead' months back to life. February was named after the festival of purification *Februa*, and January recalled the god Janus, a strange figure with two faces, looking both forwards and backwards at the same time. Clearly, given Janus's credentials, the Etruscans had intended January to be the first month of the year, but the assimilation of the Etruscan civilisation into the Roman system resulted in the postponement of this idea for several centuries.

THE CLOUDS OF CONSTABLE

10 *June* 2006 ∿

John Constable was fortunate as painters go. Born in Suffolk 230 years ago tomorrow, on 11 June 1776, he was the son of a relatively wealthy miller who hoped his son would join the family business. Young John's ambitions, however, lay elsewhere, and the lad was sent to study at the Royal Academy in London. Recognition was slow to come at first, but when three of Constable's paintings received rapturous acclaim at the Paris

Salon in 1824, his reputation was assured. That, combined with the incidental benefits of an inheritance of £20,000, allowed him to concentrate on painting landscapes for the remainder of his life.

Constable recognised the weather as an integral part of painting, and his skies in particular were the product of a lifetime's study. Indeed, he turned landscape painting on its head; rather than the landscape itself dominating the picture, as it had done for nearly all his predecessors, Constable made the sky, as he put it, 'the keynote, the standard of scale, and the chief organ of sentiment' of all his later works.

'I have done a good deal of skying lately,' he wrote to a friend in October 1821. 'I am determined to conquer all difficulties and that most arduous one among the rest. The landscape painter who does not make his skies a very material part of his compositions neglects to avail himself of one of his greatest aids.' In fact, during the summers of 1821 and 1822, Constable devoted himself almost exclusively to clouds and produced a series of detailed oil sketches, some fifty of which remain extant; each one is carefully inscribed with the time of day, the direction of the wind, and other memoranda relevant to the weather at the time.

Constable's clouds are scientifically accurate and excel in their dynamic quality, incorporating always a subtle intimation of continuing change. He was also one of the earliest painters to recognise the influence of topography on the shapes of clouds. It may be that his expertise on skies owes something to his known familiarity with the work of Luke Howard, a contemporary meteorologist who devised the scientific system of cloud classification still in use today. In any event, because he learned his craft so carefully in this respect, Constable is viewed approvingly by meteorologists.

Yet, even meteorologically, Constable's *oeuvre* was strangely limited in scope. He confined himself to simple rustic themes, mostly in the southeast of England and depicted always in the summer season; snow, ice or frost were taboo. Moreover—in contrast to

Turner, for example—visibility in Constable's paintings is nearly always good; he rarely painted mist or fog, and his horizons can be clearly seen. Oddly, although he painted a multitude of showery scenes showing well-developed cumulonimbus clouds, Constable has no known example of a cumulonimbus that had reached the decadent 'anvil' stage of its development.

THE SCIENCE OF SPIN

12 *June* 2006 ∿

King James III of Scotland, we are told, decreed in 1479 that football should be utterly cryed down. My sentiments exactly! But while my antipathy to the game stems from its current sheer ubiquity, James's reasons were more pertinent, even from today's perspective. At that time football was more of a riot than a sport; it was an amusement indulged in by opposing factions irrespective of their numbers, the only object being to drive the ball as far as possible into the zone defended by the opposition. Civil disorder, chaos, injury and even death were not uncommon at such contests, which may cause some to mutter *'Plus ça change!'*

One can assuage one's footballphobia somewhat by contemplating the aerodynamics of the game. It can be observed, for example, that a football does not always follow a straight line from the player's boot into the goalmouth; sometimes it describes a graceful curve. The trick, it seems, is to kick the ball off-centre; if the point of impact is, say, slightly to the right, it will impart to the ball an anticlockwise spin, as looked at from above.

This means that throughout its trajectory, the right-hand side of the spinning ball is moving against the flow of air streaming past it at a speed comprising, not just the forward motion of the ball itself, but also the added element of spin. The opposite happens at the left-hand side of the ball; the forward speed, relative to the air, is *reduced* by the presence of the spin. The result is a slight *increase* in air pressure on the right-hand side of the spinning ball, and *lower* pressure on the left, which combine to cause a gradual swerving to the left.

On the other hand, if the ball has been kicked exceptionally hard, but still in such a way as to acquire a spin, its high velocity at first causes the flow of air past it to break down in turbulence. In this case, the mechanism described above does not occur; it happens only when the ball has slowed down towards the end of its journey, and the airflow around the ball has become 'smooth'. The swerve, which then occurs only towards the end of the ball's trajectory, results in what I am told is a 'banana ball'.

The swerving free kick apparently first became popular in South America. Until the 1960s, the leather footballs then in use were prone to absorbing water, and the consequent increase in weight made them unresponsive in rainy weather to the aerodynamic forces caused by spin; this was not the case, however, in the warm, dry conditions common in Brazil and Argentina. It was only when footballs with a synthetic, impermeable surface became available that the technique of imparting spin, and therefore a swerve, to the ball became possible in Europe's wetter climate.

CAPTURING THE EXTREMES OF TEMPERATURE

13 *June* 2006 ～

On any particular day, two temperature values stand out as being by far the most interesting: the highest and the lowest. Indeed, apart from their intrinsic interest, the maximum and minimum are used to calculate the *average* temperature for the day—we simply add them together and divide by two. And this average in turn is used to compute the mean temperature for the month, and later for the year.

Now one way of finding, say, the highest temperature of the day would be for an observer to keep a constant eye on the thermometer, making sure to spot the precise instant when it hits its highest point. But this method demands a toll from the observer which corresponds exactly to the price of liberty. Luckily, there are easier ways.

A *thermograph* is one solution, since it provides a continuous record of the temperature on a paper chart. The traditional thermograph works on the principle that metal expands when it is heated and contracts again as it cools; the activating mechanism is a metal spiral which coils and uncoils with the variations in temperature, and this action is used to control the movement of a recording pen. More modern thermographs make use of the fact that the electrical resistance of a piece of metal changes with variations in its temperature. Either way, by examining the rising and falling trace provided by the thermograph, the maximum and minimum temperature to occur in any given period can easily be deduced.

When human observers are to hand for daily readings, however, the use of 'maximum' and 'minimum' thermometers is preferred because of the greater accuracy that they provide. The maximum thermometer is similar to the conventional thermometer, but has a narrow constriction near the bulb to impede the flow of mercury. The instrument is mounted horizontally, and as the temperature rises through each day the thermal expansion of the mercury in the bulb is sufficient to force it through the narrow opening until the highest temperature is reached. But when the temperature begins to fall again, there is no pressure on the fluid to force it back past the constriction; the mercury column breaks, and the instrument continues to register the value of the highest temperature it has experienced.

The minimum thermometer contains alcohol instead of mercury, mainly because of the former's much lower freezing point. Immersed in the fluid is a light, dumb-bell shaped object called an 'index', which is free to slide along the thermometer tube. As the temperature falls during the night and the spirit contracts, the fluid drags the index with it until the lowest value is reached. But as the temperature rises again, the expanding column of alcohol leaves the index behind at the lowest point—providing a clear 'marker' to identify the lowest temperature.

THE WEATHERPEOPLE BORROWED ALLBUTT'S KINK

14 *June* 2006 ∿

How clever these weatherpeople are, you must have thought to yourself yesterday while skimming through this column. It described, you may recall, how the thermometer used to capture the maximum temperature each day has a narrow constriction near the bulb to impede the flow of mercury. As the temperature rises, the thermal expansion of the mercury in the bulb is sufficient to force it through the narrow opening until the highest temperature is reached; but when the temperature begins to fall again, there is no pressure on the fluid to force it back past the constriction, and so the instrument continues to register the value of the highest temperature experienced since it was last reset.

'*O imitatores, servum pecus!*' might have been a more appropriate response—Horace's cry 'O imitators, what a slavish herd you are!' from *Ars Poetica*. Meteorologists have merely sequestered one of the features of the classic clinical thermometer to serve their ends.

The connection between illness and body temperature had been observed as early as 1625 by an Italian physician called Sanctorius. Gabriel Dante Fahrenheit, for example, knew all about it; in 1724 he based one of the fixed points on his temperature scale to coincide—inaccurately as it turned out—with the normal temperature of the human body, but warned that a higher value would be registered 'if the temperature of a person suffering from fever or some other disease is to be taken'. This phenomenon seems to have been largely ignored in medical circles, however, until around the middle of the nineteenth century when Dr Karl August Wunderlich in Germany pioneered the use of frequent checks on body temperature to provide an indicator of the course of a disease.

With this resurgence of interest, a practical difficulty became apparent. Doctors had to use large and cumbersome thermometers to monitor the progress of their feverish patients, instruments that could take up to twenty minutes to register the correct temperature. There was also the added problem for even the most nimble and careful of physicians that the registered temperature might well have changed before the reading could be noted.

Both problems were solved by the clinical thermometer, designed by Dr Thomas Clifford Allbutt in 1866. Since the variation of the body's temperature is limited, the clinical thermometer does not need to have a large range; it is sufficient for it to have a scale with runs from, say, 35°C to 42°C, which allows for compactness of design. And Allbutt's instrument also incorporated a clever device to capture the temperature of a patient long enough for it to be observed accurately and recorded; it had a small bend or constriction in the tube that prevented the mercury from returning to the bulb, allowing a doctor ample time to take a reading.

THE BRIGHT SIDE OF MOUNT PINATUBO

15 June 2006 ～

Until a decade and a half ago, Mount Pinatubo on the island of Luzon in the Philippines was a little-known and peaceful forest-covered mountain. Its slopes supported a population of several thousand people, mainly comprising an indigenous community, the Aeta, who had been obliged to flee from the lowlands when the Spanish conquered the region in 1565.

But Mount Pinatubo was volcanic, and after 500 years of dormancy it erupted explosively 15 years ago today, on 15 June 1991. A successful prediction of this climactic happening allowed the evacuation of tens of thousands of people from surrounding areas, and although several hundred lost their lives in the event, casualties were much lower than they might have been. Large areas of countryside, however, were covered with debris, and the volcano also injected vast quantities of smoke, ash and other pollutants into the atmosphere, which in due course distributed themselves worldwide as a layer of tiny particles high above the Earth. This injection of aerosols produced a haze of sulphuric acid droplets, thought to have been the greatest such occurrence since the eruption of Krakatoa in 1883.

But the eruption of Pinatubo was also, literally, an 'acid test' for the climate models of the time—those that had been predicting a gradual increase in global temperature because of the continuous infusion of greenhouse gases into the atmosphere. A layer of particles of this kind prevents some of the Sun's radiation from reaching the ground, and the models predicted that this should bring a temporary reversal of the global warming trend, and a drop in global temperature for the following few years. If the predicted fall in temperature occurred, it would be an indication that the computer models were working well, and could be trusted; if it did not, the forecast long-term global warming would be highly suspect.

The downward blip arrived perfectly on cue. Many regions of the world experienced a drop in average temperature in 1992 of around 0.5°C, compared to the 30-year average; later analysis also suggested that the cold, snowy weather in New Zealand late that same year, the severe damage caused by hurricanes like Iniki and Andrew, and the heavy rains in the American Midwest in the summer of 1993, were all linked to the atmospheric effects of the eruption of Mount Pinatubo.

Of course, as we know, the rise in average global temperature resumed a few years later as the atmosphere recovered, and has continued almost unabated ever since. But at least, with the help of Pinatubo, the credibility of the climate models had been much enhanced, and advocates of the greenhouse warming theories had been spared, for the time being at any rate, what T.H. Huxley

called 'the great tragedy of Science: the slaying of a beautiful
hypothesis by an ugly fact'.

THE LAKE THAT NEARLY OVERFLOWED

16 *June* 2006 ∿

L ong after the dust had literally settled, and the climatic
effects of the volcano had all died away, Mount Pinatubo
delivered another unexpected threat to local residents.
The eruption in June 1991 had left, unsurprisingly, a vast crater
on the summit of the mountain; it became apparent in due
course, however, that this seemingly innocent depression might
ultimately constitute a hazard almost as dangerous as the big
bang itself.

Annual rainfall in the Philippines region is high, at around
3,500 mm. Consequently, the crater left after the eruption began
steadily to fill with rainwater, its level rising by about a metre
every month. At first the lake was small, hot and highly acidic,
with a pH value of two and a temperature of about 40°C; the lava
dome formed a nice little island in the middle. As the years went
by, however, the Pinatubo lake got bigger and deeper, and the
added rain cooled and diluted the body of water, lowering the
temperature to 26°C and raising the pH to 5.5. But by 2001, the
lake contained 250 million cubic metres of water, and was very
close to overflowing; there was now a real danger that the sides of
the crater might collapse, suddenly releasing an avalanche of

water and mud to inundate the reoccupied towns and villages below.

The government of the Philippines ordered a controlled draining of the lake, and some 9,000 people were once again evacuated from surrounding areas in case a flood was accidentally triggered. In August 2001 vulcanologists started digging a channel adjacent to the lowest point on the crater's rim. The idea was that once a small amount of water had begun to pass along the channel, it would quickly erode the walls, enlarge the channel and increase the flow, allowing the lake water to recede to a safer level. The workers had completed their task by 7 September, and on that day only a small plug of rock remained to be blasted out of the way to allow the controlled deluge to commence.

The operation was only partially successful. The channel, it seems, was not designed as skilfully as might have been, so the initial flow of water was more of a trickle than a flood. Then the rock in the vicinity turned out to be harder than anticipated, so the expected widening of the channel by erosion did not happen. But after some remedial work, enough water was released to remove the immediate danger, and in due course about a quarter of the lake's volume was successfully drained. Moreover, the fact that the rock had turned out to be harder than was thought made a catastrophic breach less likely in the future. In any event, the local people were allowed back into their homes, and life, more or less, settled back to normal.

THE FATAL FUNGUS OF
THE GREAT FAMINE

19 *June* 2006 ∾

The potato was introduced to Ireland around 1585, thrived in the Irish climate, and became by the middle of the nineteenth century effectively the sole source of nourishment for the vast majority of the population. By that point, failure of the crop must bring catastrophe. And it came, as we know, in the years following 1845.

The culprit was potato blight, a fungal disease whose spread is directly related to very specific atmospheric conditions. *Phytophtora infestans* is highly sensitive to temperature, and its spread from plant to plant requires a film of moisture on the leaf; the longer this film persists, the greater the opportunity for infection. It has been found that the ideal conditions are a relative humidity greater than around 90 per cent, and temperature in excess of about 10°C, both existing simultaneously over an extended period.

Such weather was commonplace in northern Europe in the early summer of 1845. The blight first appeared in Belgium in late June that year; by mid-August it had spread to the south of England and it arrived in Ireland in September. The situation here caused concern but not panic, since three-quarters of the potato crop was safely harvested.

The Horsemen of the Apocalypse lay dormant for the winter but resumed their work with ruthless efficiency during the following year. On continental Europe and in Britain the summer of 1846 was dry and hot, and so the blight died out, but the Irish weather collaborated cruelly. From late July onwards, just when the all-important potato plants were reaching their maturity, it was abnormally wet and warm. The first sign of the resurgent disease was a pervasive, tell-tale stench of decay which permeated the air even when the stalks remained deceptively luxuriant; it was followed by livid patches on the leaves, which advanced until the stem became a putrid mass; by early August the fields were black with rotting plants and the season's crop was an almost total loss.

The sudden onslaught was described by Father Theobald Mathew, the legendary Apostle of Temperance, in a letter dated 7 August 1846, to Sir Charles Trevelyan, the Secretary to the Treasury responsible for such relief measures as there were: 'On 27th of last month, I passed from Cork to Dublin and this doomed plant bloomed in all the luxuriance of an abundant harvest. Returning on 3rd instant, however, I beheld with sorrow one wide waste of putrefying vegetation. In many places the wretched people were seated on the fences of their decaying gardens, wringing their hands and bewailing bitterly this destruction that had left them foodless.'

The population of the island, which had been rising steadily before the Famine, dropped by two million people, or more than 20 per cent, because of the combined effects of death and emigration. The demographic consequences of the event have shaped Ireland's history ever since.

THE ORIGINAL BLACK HOLE OF CALCUTTA

20 *June* 2006 ∿

Certain events in history acquire a notoriety quite dispro-portionate to their intrinsic importance at the time. One such was the incarceration, with fatal results, of a small group of British prisoners in Calcutta 250 years ago today, on the night of 20 June 1756.

Earlier that year, the Nawab of Bengal became unhappy with the influence of the British East India Company in the region, perceiving it as a threat to his dominion. He laid siege to Calcutta, and when the city ultimately fell, captives were placed for the night in the company's local lock-up for petty offenders, popularly known as the Black Hole.

A contemporary historian takes up the story: 'On one of the hottest of the hot nights in British India, Sarij Uddaula, a youthful merciless ruler of Bengal, caused to be confined within a small cell 146 Englishmen whom he had that day captured in a siege of the city of Calcutta. The room was large enough to house comfortably but two persons. Its heavy door was bolted; its walls were pierced by two windows barred with iron through which little air could enter.'

Now, four major changes take place in the air of an enclosed space as a result of human occupation. By their collective breath-ing, the crowd reduces the oxygen content of the air and increases the proportion of carbon dioxide it contains; in addition, body heat from the assembled humans increases the temperature inside the room, and the moisture of their exhalations brings about a rise in the humidity. As we shall see, the combination, taken to extremes, may well be lethal:

Within a few minutes every man was bathed in a wet perspiration and was striving to escape the stifling heat. The dungeon became the scene of terrible strugglings, as the steaming mass of sentient human bodies vied for the insufficient air. Clothing was soon stripped off, breathing became difficult, and there were vain onslaughts on the windows and attempts to force the door.

Thirst grew intolerable and men became delirious. Those who fell to the floor faced certain death for they were crushed and buried beneath the desperate wave of frenzied humanity above. The night passed slowly, and with the advent of morning death had come to all but a score of the luckless company.

This tragedy of the Black Hole of Calcutta will ever remain as the most drastic demonstration in human history of the bondage of man to the air by which he is surrounded.

The affair is also recalled as one of the most callous acts in human history, although more recent evidence suggests that the Nawab's crime may have been the rather lesser one of unintended negligence. In any event, the incident became a focus of indignation for the entire western world, and an important catalyst towards the evolution of the British Raj in India.

THE DISCOURSE OF LOUGH DOON

28 June 2006 ～

Geologists of the early nineteenth century had great difficulty explaining the existence all over Europe of gigantic boulders which differed in composition from their surroundings, and had obviously been transported to their location from a distant spot. The generally accepted explanation was that these erratics, as they were called, were carried to their destinations by the great currents of water and mud assumed to have accompanied Noah's flood.

One Jean de Charpentier, however, a mining engineer who worked in Switzerland, thought differently. In 1834 he became the first to suggest that there might be a tide in the affairs of men—a tide of ice whose ebb and flow takes half a million years, and which scooped up giant rocks as it advanced only to deposit them in splendid isolation several hundred miles from their point of origin.

No one paid much attention to de Charpentier, but the new idea was championed by a 27-year-old professor of Natural History at the University of Neuchâtel called Louis Agazziz. In July 1837 Agazziz gave a seminal lecture on the topic to a meeting of the Swiss Society of Natural Sciences, remembered as 'The Discourse of Neuchâtel'; it began a dispute—one of the most acrimonious in the history of science—that was to rage for more than a quarter of a century, ending with the universal acceptance of the ice-age theory.

Agazziz visited Ireland in 1840 and identified several landscapes in Cavan, Down and Dublin that illustrated his theory, but to most of the local pundits the existence of an ice age, Irish or otherwise, remained, at best, an open question.

It was John Ball who clinched the argument for Ireland in 1849. Ball was a 30-year-old Dubliner who had graduated from Cambridge and then spent several years on the Continent studying natural history. On his travels, he saw the glaciers of Switzerland and became familiar with the controversial theories of de Charpentier and Agazziz. In 1846 he had returned to Ireland, become a Poor Law Commissioner, and was posted to County Kerry to supervise measures for famine relief.

Everywhere Ball looked in County Kerry, he saw signs of ancient glacial activity that were similar to those of more recent origin in Switzerland. He noticed in particular Lough Doon, a small, unassuming and secluded body of water that lies in a deep hollow in the Dingle Mountains near the Connor Pass, and it was this he chose as his most spectacular exemplar of the action of the ice. In November 1849 Ball presented his theories on the characteristics of Lough Doon and its surroundings to the Geological Society of Dublin in a lecture entitled 'Notice of the Former Existence of Small Glaciers in the County of Kerry', thereby irrefutably establishing the ice-age theory in Ireland.

A FLASH FLOOD IN COUNTY LEITRIM

29 June 2006 ∾

The flooding we are most familiar with in Ireland occurs when heavy and continuous rain occurs for an extended period, gradually drowning the landscape over a wide area and accumulating well beyond the carrying capacity of the local rivers. Less frequent, and different in character, is flooding brought about by a very localised but severe thundery downpour suddenly depositing millions of tons of water on terrain that, for a while at any rate, just cannot cope. It is well known in other countries as a 'flash flood'.

Flash floods occur most frequently in regions that enjoy long periods of dry weather, but are prone also to occasional, very heavy thunderstorms. A parched landscape is quickly overwhelmed by a torrent of water sweeping along its surface. But another reason why an area may react quickly to a sudden downpour is that it is already saturated, so that additional heavy rain runs off immediately, rather than being absorbed readily into the soil.

Such an event took place twenty years ago today, on the morning of 29 June 1986, in the catchment of the Yellow River, which flows westwards from the Iron Mountains in County Leitrim into Lough Allen on the upper reaches of the Shannon. The river rapidly overflowed its banks, filling the flood plain with water and significantly altering the course of the river itself. More importantly, perhaps, the heavy rains caused a series of landslides, stripping a carpet of peat more than a metre thick from the underlying rock of the surrounding hillsides and shifting it downslope by several hundred metres. The event was the subject of a detailed study shortly after its occurrence by Dr Pete Coxon of TCD and several of his colleagues.

The immediate trigger was a downpour during the night of 28/29 June. A raingauge at Aughnasheelin, near the centre of the area of interest, recorded 111 millimetres of rain, the great bulk of which is reckoned to have fallen during an hour or two around 1am. This makes the rainfall comparable in intensity to that of the memorable Merrion rainstorm in Dublin in June 1963, when 80 mm, or more than 3 inches, fell in the course of a single hour.

Of crucial importance to the consequences of the Yellow River downpour, however, was the fact that although the weather had been dry for several weeks beforehand, the rain of 28/29 June was preceded by a smaller but significant fall on 27 June. It seems likely that this, while no threat for flooding on its own, was sufficient to correct the moisture deficit in the soil which had accumulated during the dry spell. When the second downpour came, therefore, it fell on ground already saturated; the soil could absorb no more water, and the excess streamed freely and rapidly down the hillsides with dramatic consequences.

THE ELEMENTS AT WAR

1 *July* 2006 ∽

M y grandfather, Robert Smyth, was at the Somme. He was a 25-year-old telephone technician in his native Derry when he joined up as sapper in the Royal Engineers. In his later years he talked about the lighter side of those youthful days in France, proud throughout his life of the military training which translated into mild admonishments in my direction: 'Pull up your socks, straighten your tie, young fella; that's no way to be going on parade.'

But he never spoke of the darker side of that experience, and undoubtedly, for him as for everybody else, there was a darker side. Once, when I was 14, I asked him why he had gone to war, and I remember clearly the slightly wistful tone of his response. 'I was imbued', he said, 'with a spirit of patriotism.' It was an uncharacteristically philosophical turn of phrase for a sensitive but essentially very simple man, and I was too young, to my subsequent regret, to enquire further. In any event, young Robert survived to marry my grandmother in 1919—proudly in his uniform—and resumed his happy but mundane existence as a post-office technician in another foreign country, Caherciveen.

That great conflict left its legacy to meteorology as well. Around that time, meteorologists in Norway were beginning to understand the genesis of a depression, and central to their theory was a sharp discontinuity that stretched across the North Atlantic, a semi-permanent transition zone in the mid-latitudes separating the cold polar air-mass from the temperate westerlies farther south. They were struck by the analogy with the two great armies, roughly balanced in size, currently facing each other along a zigzag line of trenches stretching from the North Sea down to Switzerland.

Despite minor incursions costing hundreds of thousands of lives apiece, the battle lines of World War I swayed only a few miles to and fro along the entire length of the Western Front. The confrontation of the Atlantic air masses was reminiscent of this conflict. Here, too, minor disturbances occurred from time to time along the dividing line, incursions of warm, humid air into the colder northern territory, or *vice versa*. It seemed natural to the Norwegians to call the discontinuity they had discovered, the dividing line between the different kinds of air, a 'front'—the polar front.

By this analogy, the familiar 'warm sector' of a depression can be seen in military terms as a major invasion into enemy territory, as the battle of the Somme was hoped to be. Each belt of rain that crosses Ireland signals a temporary victory for the mellow southern air, which is followed shortly afterwards by a counter-attack from the north, in the shape of the cold, blustery, northwesterly winds sweeping down behind the low.

There are no victors in this perennial battle of the elements, nor has there ever been an armistice.

A FORECASTER OF DOOM AND GLOOM

3 *July* 2006 〜

'He was slightly less than middle height, robustly cheerful and vigorous; his brow was high and open, the nose straight, and the grey eyes gentle; his beard was thick and his health, even in old age, was good.' Thus did his assistant, Jean de Chavigny, describe Michel de Nostre Dame, better known to history as simply Nostradamus.

He was born near Avignon in southern France in December 1503, and trained as a physician, becoming very successful in that profession in his younger years. In middle age, however, Nostradamus settled in the town of Salon-de-Provence and astrology became his *forte*, a discipline in which he developed, many believe, an uncanny talent as a forecaster. He specialised in long-range predictions, portraying the fate of mankind as dominated by disaster, death and horror; indeed, to a large extent, it was the tantalising fear which they instilled that led to the wide promulgation of his vague pronouncements.

These were published in a series of books collectively known as *Les Centuries*, so called because each contained 100 rhyming quatrains filled with mysterious references to alleged events that would happen in the future. Nostradamus's adherents claim, for example, that he foretold the Great Fire of London in 1666:

> *Le sang de just a Londres fera faulte,*
> *Brusles par fuoldres de vingt trois les six,*

which roughly translates as 'The blood of the just will be demanded of London, burnt by fire in three times twenty plus six.'

By his assertion that 'A great swarm of bees will arise, but no one will know whence they have come', Nostradamus is credited with predicting the *coup d'état* that brought Napoleon, whose emblem was the bee, to power. And Napoleon's banishment to Elba is allegedly foretold in the lines:

> *Le grand empire sera tost translate,*
> *En lieu petit; ou au milieu viendra poser son septre.*

'The great empire will soon be exchanged for a small place, in the middle of which he will lay down his sceptre.' There are even those nowadays who believe Nostradamus has warned us of the consequences of global warming:

> *La terre aride en siccite croistra,*
> *Et grans deluges quand sera aperceu.*

'The dry earth will grow more parched, and there will be great floods when it is seen.'

Michel de Nostre Dame, *le mage de Salon-de-Provence*, or the Seer of Salon, died 450 years ago yesterday, on 2 July 1566. One can imagine him, as his end approached, chortling to himself in terms similar to Joyce's sentiments when he had completed *Ulysses*: 'I've put in so many enigmas and puzzles that it will keep the professors busy for centuries over what I meant; that's the only way of ensuring one's immortality.'

HOW THE WORLD GOES ROUND

4 *July* 2006 ~

L ooked at from a certain point of view, today ought to be the coldest day of the entire year. This possibility arises from the fact that the path of the Earth around the Sun is an ellipse rather than a perfect circle, with the result that sometimes we are closer to the Sun than we are at others. The time of year when our planet is closest to the Sun—at *perihelion*, a 'mere' 147 million kilometres away from it—varies over thousands of years, but currently occurs during the first week in January; we are farthest from the Sun, on the other hand—at *aphelion*, 152 million kilometres distant—around now, during the first week of July.

An interesting consequence of the Earth's non-circular orbit is that the two equinoxes are not, as you might expect, exactly half a year apart. If you count up the days, you will find that it is approximately 186 days from 21 March to 23 September, and only 179 days from the autumnal to the vernal equinox again. This means, strictly speaking, that the northern hemisphere has a slightly longer summer than its southern counterpart.

The variation in distance from the Sun caused by the Earth's elliptical orbit ought also to affect the average temperature of our planet at the different times of year by a degree or two, and so indeed it does behind the scenes. Its net effect is that our winters in the northern hemisphere are milder and shorter, and our summers slightly cooler, than would be the case if the Earth travelled in a perfect circle. But another factor is much more important in governing the annual cycle of temperatures in different regions of the world.

As well as orbiting the Sun, the Earth spins like a top on its own axis. Moreover, its axis of rotation, rather than being at right angles to the plane of orbit around the Sun, is tilted from it by about 23 degrees. As our planet proceeds on its year-long journey around the Sun, the tilted axis maintains a constant orientation in space, pointing roughly at the pole star, and as a consequence, the Sun, as viewed from Earth, appears to oscillate slowly north and south of the equatorial line—causing, as it does so, the annual procession of the seasons.

During our summer, the Sun's rays shine vertically down on the lower latitudes of the northern hemisphere, maximising the daily absorption of solar radiation in our part of the world. During our winter, on the other hand, the sunshine hits the northern hemisphere at a very oblique angle; as a result, much of the radiation is reflected back to space, and that which does impinge upon the surface of the Earth is spread over a comparatively large area, diminishing its heating capabilities.

EVERYTHING IN PROPER ORDER

7 July 2006 ∿

Hamlet, as you may know, was the most verbose of all the characters in Shakespeare's dramas. He is given a total of nearly 1,600 lines to utter 'trippingly on the tongue', well ahead of the two joint seconds, Richard III, who was so famously lacking of a horse, and Iago, who helped in his subversive way to do the state some service; they had approximately a mere 1,100 lines apiece. Brutus, Romeo and Macbeth were less than half as talkative as Hamlet, while Desdemona and Cordelia Lear have, by comparison, hardly anything to say at all.

And then we have ETAINOS. This is not, as you might suspect, a Greek award for some achievement above and beyond the call of duty, but a handy little *aide-mémoire* to tell you the seven most common letters of the English alphabet. Thus, e is used most often, followed by t, a, i, n, o and s in decreasing frequency. H and r, on the other hand, are used only half as much as e, while down at the very bottom of the list lie k, q, j and x, and finally, the most shunned letter of the alphabet, the z.

You can play little games like this in meteorology. In Dublin, for example, the wettest month of the year, on average, is December. The second wettest, which may well surprise you, is the month of August, explained by the fact that August weather is often rather thundery in character; the duration of the rain may be relatively short compared to other months, but the rain when it does come is often heavy and thundery, with large amounts falling in short periods. August is followed in terms of wetness by September, November, January, October and July, in that order. April is the driest Dublin month in terms of total rainfall, followed in turn by March and June.

This regime is fairly typical of Leinster and east Ulster, but over in the west of the country the pattern is more regular and less surprising. It shows, in general, a wet part of the year from September on to January inclusive, with significantly less rain in the seven months from February through August.

You can have further fun, if you have nothing else to do, by putting summers and winters of the twentieth century in their proper order. There are many contenders, for example, for the worst winter of the century; the favourites for the title are 1909/10, 1916/17, 1932/33, 1946/47, 1962/63, 1978/79, and 1981/82, all of which had periods of widespread and disruptive snow. The best summers, on the other hand, in recent times at any rate, are reckoned to have been 1975, 1976, 1983, 1989 and, of course, most memorably, 1995. And the bad ones? They were probably 1985, 1986 and 1993, and the very mediocre summer of 1996.

THE VERDICT OF THIS COURT . . .

8 *July* 2006 ∽

The saga about human involvement in climatic change might be said to have begun in the summer of 1988 when a NASA scientist called James Hansen outlined to a Congressional hearing in the United States his views on the then novel topic of the greenhouse effect on global climate. Many scientists were shocked by the sensational media reports that followed, and felt that it was premature to conclude that we humans had anything to do with global warming. It became a case of, as Horace puts it, *grammatici certant et adhuc sub judice lis est*: 'The scholars argue amongst themselves and the case is still before the courts.'

Insofar as there was any court to adjudicate on such an issue, it came to be the Intergovernmental Panel on Climate Change. The IPCC was a standing committee of international experts established in 1988 by the World Meteorological Organization and the United Nations Environment Programme. The Panel comprised several hundred of the world's leading experts on such matters, and it was charged with arriving at a reliable and unprejudiced consensus, an authoritative 'best guess', on what was happening. Was humanity guilty of crimes against humanity—or not?

So far the court has issued three verdicts in the form of its 1990, 1995 and 2001 reports, and it is interesting to review the development of its jurisprudence. In 1990 the IPCC was cautious; the experts confirmed that the average temperature of our planet had increased by half a degree or so in the previous century, but stressed that this increase was within the bounds of 'natural climatic variability'. It might have happened anyway, the IPCC said; its verdict was essentially 'innocent until proven guilty'.

After consideration of the evidence that came before it during the following five years, however, there was a decisive shift in the opinion of the court. In 1995 the IPCC reported that 'the balance of evidence suggests a discernible human influence on global climate'. This time their verdict on humanity was 'guilty on the balance of probability'.

Then six years later, in 2001, the Panel concluded that the increase in global temperature in recent times was 'unprecedented in the last 10,000 years', and could be plausibly explained *only* by taking account of human influence. It further concluded that other factors affecting the global climate—changes in radiant solar energy, or volcanic dust thrown into the atmosphere from time to time—should have made the world cooler, not warmer, during the previous two decades. Clearly the verdict of the court was 'guilty beyond all reasonable doubt'.

The IPCC will produce its next report in 2007. On this occasion it seems likely that the guilt of the accused will be confirmed without leave to appeal. The preoccupation of the court will be 'victim impact assessment': how bad will things really be in this brave new greenhouse world?

THE TROUBLE WITH GLACIERS

10 *July* 2006 ⌒

You may have noticed from newspaper reports that the eastern flank of the Eiger mountain in Switzerland is in imminent danger of collapse. The finger of suspicion, as invariably in recent times, points accusingly at global warming.

The theory is that the Grindelwald glacier at the foot of the mountain has played a major part for centuries in shoring up the Eiger's eastern face. The glacier has been retreating for many decades, recently by up to a metre every year and, deprived of its support, the Eiger now displays a crack of over four metres, which is widening alarmingly. It has been predicted that perhaps sometime during the coming week around two million cubic metres of solid rock will cascade down the mountainside onto the retreating glacier some 200 metres below. Spectators have apparently gathered in large numbers to watch the fun.

The Swiss are always having trouble with their glaciers. Back in 1644, for example, the problem was an advancing glacier rather than a retreating one. At that time, Europe was in the grip of the so-called Little Ice Age, a period of very cold conditions which lasted from about 1450 until the middle of the nineteenth century. During it, Alpine farmers suffered greatly from advances by the glaciers, and the folklore of the region is rich in tales of ice from the mountain fastnesses overwhelming the previously green and fertile valleys down below. Moreover, in very cold conditions a glacier might sometimes put on a sudden spurt, and it required only a small leap of the imagination for local people to believe in such circumstance that the ice had become possessed by evil spirits from the Alps.

This was what happened at Chamonix in the summer of 1644. Not far outside the town,

> *The ice was here, the ice was there,*
> *The ice was all around;*
> *It cracked and growled, and roared and howled,*
> *Like noises in a swound!*

The *des Bossons* glacier was on the move. 'The noise of the surge was heard at a distance of two to three kilometres. The margin advanced at about one metre per hour in a kind of rhythmic movement, with one small advance every second or so. Each intermittent advance could be seen and heard, and was accompanied by a palpable shivering of the ground.' The ice threatened to engulf the town.

The townspeople, however, devised a very effective remedy. They asked the local bishop, his Lordship of Geneva, to exorcise the ice, and on a bright Sunday morning he led a procession to the glacier's snout and performed the necessary ritual. His Lordship was either well connected up in heaven, or very lucky here on earth. In any event, Chamonix survived; in time, the average temperature of the region recovered with the ending of the Little Ice Age, and the Alpine glaciers retreated to their present limits.

YE WINDS OF DIFFERING FAITHS

12 July 2006 ∼

In the autumn of 1688, a certain song was much in vogue among adherents to the House of Orange. Bishop Gilbert Burnet, a staunch supporter of Prince William, made mention of it in his memoirs: 'A foolish ballad was made at that time, treating the Papists, and chiefly the Irish, in a ridiculous manner, which had a burden *ero lero lilibulero* and that made an impression on the army that cannot be well imagined by those that saw it not. The people both in the city and the country were singing it perpetually.'

The song was *Lilliburlero*, and it includes a verse which runs:

> *Oh, but why does he stay behind?*
> *Lilliburlero Bullenala.*
> *Ho, by my soul, 'tis a Protestant wind;*
> *Lilliburlero Bullenala.*

The refrain, meaningless at first sight, is said to be Gaelic, and a corruption of An lile ba léir é, ba linn an lá—'The lily will win out, the day will be ours'—the orange lily, of course, being the symbol of the House of Orange. But what does 'the Protestant wind' signify?—apart from suggesting that the word 'wind' was pronounced differently in those days than it is now.

William at the time was still in Holland. King James II occupied the throne of England, but was not, to put it mildly, a universally popular monarch. Indeed, kingship seemed to go to his head somewhat, and many of his subjects felt the need to look elsewhere for a more reasonable incumbent for the throne. The obvious choice was William, Prince of Orange, a nephew of King James, and as it happened, also the husband of his daughter Mary. William accepted the invitation, and plans were laid—not for an invasion—but for what was euphemistically referred to throughout the whole episode as William's 'descent' upon England.

There was, however, one important prerequisite. The Prince's armada could not sail from the Netherlands without the help of an easterly wind, and for many weeks the weather was singularly unobliging. As the historian Thomas Babington Macaulay described it: 'The gales which at times blew obstinately from the west prevented the Prince's armament from sailing, and also brought fresh Irish regiments from Dublin to Chester, where they were bitterly cursed and reviled by the common people. The weather, it was said, "is Popish". Crowds stood in Cheapside gazing intently at the weather-cock on the graceful steeple of Bow Church, praying for a Protestant wind.'

The Popish wind blew stiff and strong for many weeks. It was 11 November 1688 before the Protestant wind finally arrived, and William of Orange was able to fulfil his destiny by setting sail for England, a journey that was to culminate in the Battle of the Boyne on 1 July—or 12 July by our Gregorian Calendar—1690.

APRIL, COME SHE WILL . . .

13 *July* 2006 ⌒

Sir John Rogerson's Quay in Dublin lies opposite the Point Depot. The eponymous Sir John was Lord Mayor of Dublin in 1693/94, and in 1716 he built the quay wall that bears his name, reclaiming the mudflats behind it and thereby, no doubt, adding substantially to his already considerable fortune. If you happen to be passing Sir John Rogerson's Quay today you may notice a battleship attached thereto, a French vessel of the frigate class called *Germinal*, here to celebrate Bastille Day, *le Quatorze Juillet*, tomorrow.

Now the ship's name, *Germinal*, may ring only the tiniest of bells. But if I tell you that the frigate has a quintet of sister ships called *Floréal*, *Prairial*, *Nivose*, *Ventose* and *Vendémiaire* you will recognise them instantly as the months of the Republican Calendar used in France for 13 years from 1792. 'We cannot go on reckoning the years as we did when we were oppressed by kings,' the National Convention was told on 24 October 1793 by Philippe Fabre d'Eglantine: 'Every page of the Gregorian calendar is soiled by the prejudices and falsehoods of the throne and Church.' The Convention duly agreed and the new calendar was adopted, backdated to 22 September 1792, so that the day following the official abolition of the monarchy, and coincidentally the autumn equinox, was deemed to have been the first day of Year I of the Republic.

The months of the five frigates listed above were those of Flowers, Meadows, Snow, Wind and the Harvest of the Grape respectively; *Germinal* was the month of Seeds, the 30 days beginning on what had previously been 21 March. The names of the full twelve—devised, it is said, by Fabre d'Eglantine himself—

reflected their climatic or agricultural significance in the scheme of things. The seven-day week was abandoned, and each new month was divided into three *decades*, while the ten days of each week were styled, with admirable logic, *primidi*, *duodi* and so on up to *decadi*, this last being a day of rest in place of Sunday.

Just as each day in the old calendar had its saint, every day in the new arrangement was dedicated to an animal, a vegetable or agricultural implement, and some enthusiastic anti-Christians changed their names to match the items now honoured on their old name-day—but not everyone; even the most ardent François might hesitate to become Potiron, or Pumpkin, after the vegetable to which St Francis's Day was now dedicated; and Catherine, by the same logic, was likely to find a change of name to 'Pig' to be too revolutionary by far.

Poor Fabre d'Eglantine, alas, received little thanks for his imaginative efforts. Only a few months after the adoption of his calendar he incurred the wrath of Robespierre; he was arrested in early 1794 and perished on the guillotine on 5 April, or 16 *Germinal*, Year II.

A WEATHER PRECURSOR TO A REVOLUTION

14 *July* 2006 ～

'Est-ce une révolte?' enquired Louis XVI of the duc de La Rochefoucauld-Liancourt. *'Non, Sire,'* came the reply, *'c'est un révolution.'* Today, *le Quatorze Juillet*, is the anniversary of that apocryphal conversation, a day that commemorates a turning point in French history, and indeed in the history of the world: the fall of the Bastille in Paris in 1789.

The many causes of the French Revolution have been exhaustively documented down the years, but it is clear that weather played a part. Poor harvests, owing to lack of rain, were a common feature of the eighteenth century in France, but 1788 was worst of all; an exceptionally warm spring began a summer which turned out to be the driest of the decade, and the harvest promised to be the worst for many years. The last straw was an unusual meteorological event on 13 July that year, twelve months almost to the day before the Bastille fell. A violent summer thunderstorm rained giant hailstones over northern France and the hardships that ensued inflamed the anger of a hungry populace.

Weather reports came from the most unlikely sources. The storm was of such proportions that a few days later the British Ambassador to France, Lord Dorset, dispatched a comprehensive description of it to his Foreign Secretary in London:

> A storm of thunder, lightning and hail experienced in the environs of Paris last Sunday morning was uncommonly violent and has done much mischief in those parts. The hailstones were of a size and weight never heard of before in this country, some of them measuring sixteen inches in circumference. Near St Germain, two men were found dead upon the road, and a horse so much bruised that it was determined to kill him from a motive of humanity to put an end to his misery.
>
> The noise that was heard in the air previous to the falling of the immense hailstones is said to have been beyond all description dreadful. It is impossible to give expression to the damage that has been done. Some of the largest trees were torn up by the roots, all the corn and vines destroyed, windows broken and even some houses broken down. It is computed that from

twelve to fifteen hundred villages have suffered more or less damage.

A poor harvest had been expected even before this catastrophe occurred. But the hail destroyed much of the meagre supply of grain available; in due course civil disturbance, brought on by lack of food, grew commonplace throughout the realm, and in the towns and cities the high price of bread caused riots in the streets. Moreover, it was clear that peasants would be unable to pay their taxes and that the royal treasury, already in dire straits, would finally be bankrupt. The King agreed to convene the Estates General, and the rest, quite literally, is history.

SIZZLING IN THE CITY STREETS

18 *July* 2006 ∿

The weather was like this when the Indian warrior Kwasind drowned in the sluggish waters of the River Taquamenaw. Longfellow describes it in 'The Song of Hiawatha':

'Twas an afternoon in Summer;
Very hot and still the air was;
Very smooth the gliding river,
. . . . . .
Very languid with the weather,
Very sleepy with the silence.

an idyllic environment indeed in which to live one's final
moments. But that, of course, was in the country; one might even
say the wilderness. Given the same meteorological scenario, conditions in the city—if cities there had been in Hiawatha's time—
would have been very much more harsh.

There is little difference between town and country on a sunny,
summer morning. In fact, it is not unknown for the shade
temperature in the city to be a little lower than that of the
surrounding countryside in the forenoon, because of the slight
attenuation of the city sunlight by the dust and smoke endemic in
the urban atmosphere.

But city streets sizzle in the afternoon. For the pedestrian
walking the pavements in the sunshine, the intrinsic warmth of
the air is augmented by the heating effect of the direct sunlight
beating down from overhead. And more energy is reflected in his
or her direction from the brightly painted surfaces of nearby
buildings. Added to these is the fact that the incessant stream of
solar energy causes the surface temperature of streets, footpaths
and south-facing buildings to soar to perhaps 60°C or 70°C, and
all these surfaces re-radiate their heat in the direction of the
unfortunate passerby.

To make matters worse, the surrounding buildings break up
the cooling effect of any breezes that might otherwise offer some
relief. And if there happen to be showers, the efficient and very
rapid drainage of surface water in the city means that less energy
is allowed to dissipate through evaporation than if the liquid were
allowed to lie; the significant decrease in temperature which
accompanies this process in the open country is virtually absent
in the urban environment.

The brick and concrete of the buildings, and the compacted
soils beneath the city roads and parking areas, act like giant storage heaters to store their received energy efficiently. In this they
are much more effective than the relatively loose and 'air-filled'

soil of agricultural land. Although the streets and buildings start to cool as night approaches, they release their heat only very slowly during the hours of darkness—'at midnight,' as Thomas Hardy puts it, 'when the noon-heat breathes it back from walls and leads'. This prevents the city night-time temperature from falling as low as otherwise it might; by morning this excess heat has not entirely expended itself, and if the sunny spell continues, the next sizzling day begins with a 'built-in' thermal advantage— or handicap, depending on how you wish to look at it.

THE ORIGINAL MEANDER BELT

24 *July* 2006 ∽

Most large rivers have their origins in a mountain spring or lake. The stream carves out mountain gullies for itself, running swiftly down along a course that at first is reasonably straight. As it descends onto the plain below, however, and the slope of the ground becomes more gentle and nearer to the horizontal, the river broadens and its speed diminishes.

Once on relatively level ground, the river erodes laterally rather than vertically. It grinds away at its banks on either side, rather than trying to dig a deeper channel for itself. By now, flowing in a straight line is not a stable situation; the slightest deviation, the merest gentle curve, requires the water to flow more quickly on the *outside* of the bend than it does on the inside. This results in erosion of the riverbank on the outside of the curve, and deposition of material in the relatively slow-moving water on the inside. Over time, therefore, any slight bend in the river has a tendency to be enhanced; each curve becomes more and more pronounced and the river follows a 'meandering' path.

The term comes from the river Buyuk Menderes, called *Maiandros* by the ancient Greeks, which winds its way through that part of modern Turkey known to the Greeks as Phrygia. It flows into the Aegean Sea near Samos, and pursues such a very winding, sinuous course that its name has been adopted as an adjective for any waterway that shows this tendency. The Meander, apart from its celebrity as eponym, has also been immortalised by Milton in The Lady's Song from 'Comus':

> *Sweet Echo, sweetest Nymph that liv'st unseen*
> *Within thy airy shell*
> *By slow Meander's margent green,*
> *And in the violet-embroidered vale,*
> *Where the lovelorn Nightingale*
> *Nightly to thee her sad Song mourneth well.*

The best meandering occurs in river valleys where a fine-grained, cohesive soil and thriving vegetation make the outside of a bend relatively resistant to erosion. This slows the process sufficiently for deposition on the inside of a bend to keep pace with the retreating outside curve, allowing the river to maintain its coherence as it migrates, rather than just spread out into a series of untidy streams and pools. Moreover, good meanderers, rather than lashing about wildly over a large area, tend to undulate back and forth over the centuries within a well-defined strip of ground, called the 'meander-belt', defined by the terrain.

Sometimes a meander becomes so exaggerated and pronounced that only a narrow neck of land separates two adjoining portions of the river. In such a situation, when the river flows more quickly in times of flood, it may eventually cut right through this neck of land. Deposits later seal off the abandoned meander to create an isolated area of water of a horseshoe shape, a so-called 'ox-bow' lake.

A FATAL RENDEZVOUS

25 *July* 2006 ∿

Nantucket is a little island on the Massachusetts coast, a few miles off Cape Cod. Fifty years ago today two ocean liners were steaming in opposite directions in its close proximity:

Alien they seemed to be
No mortal eye could see
The intimate welding of their later history
Or sign that they were bent
By paths coincident
On being twin halves of one august event.

One of these vessels, the *Stockholm*, had just left New York on its way to Scandinavia. The other, headed for New York, was a luxurious Italian liner launched five years previously and designed 'as a living testament to the importance of beauty in the everyday world'; named after the sixteenth-century Genoese admiral who was the foremost naval commander of his time, she was called the *Andrea Doria*.

As it approached the Nantucket Lightship around 10pm on 25 July 1956, the *Stockholm* was in calm waters under an overcast sky with good visibility. Sea fog, however, is a frequent visitor to the North American coast stretching from Massachusetts up to Newfoundland, occurring when warm, moist, southerly winds, having absorbed an abundance of moisture from the Gulf Stream, find themselves suddenly over the chillier waters farther north. Through one such fogbank the *Andrea Doria* was heading southwest with engines at full speed, Captain Piero Calamai being anxious to make up time that had been lost earlier in the voyage. He was confident that the ship's powerful radar would identify other vessels in the vicinity in ample time to alter course.

And so, indeed, it did. Both vessels appeared on the other's radar, but confusion arose as to whether or not the 'Rules of the Road'—which require ships to pass each other 'port-to-port'—should apply in this particular case. Moreover Captain Curzio Franchini of the *Stockholm* assumed at first that he would be able to see the other vessel in good time as it approached, since his ship had not yet encountered any fog, although shortly afterwards it did.

At 11.06pm both ships, now in close proximity, finally sighted each other through the thickening fog and a tragic *pas-de-deux* ensued. The *Stockholm* swung to starboard, while Captain Calamai of the *Andrea Doria* called out 'All left!' and brought his ship directly into the other's path. At 11.09pm the reinforced bow of the *Stockholm* pierced the starboard side of *Andrea Doria*, inflicting a gash more than 30 feet in length.

Twelve hours later the *Andrea Doria* slipped forever beneath the surface of the North Atlantic. Better communications, and rapid response by other ships in the vicinity, averted a disaster on the scale of that of the *Titanic* in 1912, but 50 of the 1,700 souls aboard were lost. Captain Calamai survived, but he was never given another command and died shortly afterwards, a broken man.

A HAPPY CITY IN THE CLOUDS

29 *July* 2006 ∽

These days, the works of Aristophanes do not feature much upon the stage. Born about 450BC, this talented Athenian has left us about a dozen plays, all celebrated for their wittiness of dialogue, their good-natured satire and the brilliance of their sometimes cruel parody. One might be forgiven for assuming that *Clouds* must be his work of most meteorological significance, but in fact it is far surpassed in this respect by *The Birds*, a comedy first performed in Athens in 414BC and to which we are indebted for the history of that nebulous metropolis, Cloud-Cuckoo-Land.

The play is said to be a political satire on the imperialist dreams which had impelled the Athenians towards an ill-fated attempt to conquer Syracuse in Sicily in 415BC. The two main characters, Peithetairos and Euelpides, have become disenchanted with their life in Athens, frustrated by its tedious bureaucracy and lengthy intellectual arguments. They decide to move to a more congenial setting, leaving the city—and coincidentally their debts—behind. They go in search of Tereus, a character from Greek mythology whom the gods have turned into a bird, and who for various reasons they believe may have some bright ideas as to where they ought to settle down.

The three decide that, with the help of all the other birds, they will establish a city in the sky, away up in the clouds and far away from all their earthly troubles. This new city would be very powerful; its inhabitants would have the seeds of the earth available as food, but they can also intercept the fumes from the earthly sacrifices by which Zeus and all the other gods are nourished, and thus significantly weaken them. The chorus of birds, hostile at first, is finally won over to the plan, and they quickly set about building the city under the direction of Euelpides and Peithetairos—who with the help of a magic root are able to grow wings to suit their new environment.

But life in this Utopia is not without its troubles. Our heroes receive a constant stream of unwanted visitors from earth, each with problems that they hope can be solved by sojourn in the city of the clouds. Then Iris, the messenger of the gods, calls in to break her journey down to earth to find out what happened to the sacrifices; she is asked for her passport and generally made unwelcome, to the extent that she finally flies off in tears to complain to chief-god Zeus, which will undoubtedly bring trouble.

Of course the whole affair has a happy, chaotic and inconsequential ending. But the most salient point of relevance to this column is that Peithetairos and Euelpides decide to call their wonderland *Nephelokokkygia*, 'Cloud-cuckoo-land'—a term that ever since has been used to describe any impractical scheme with unrealisable Utopian ambitions.

A VOCATION FOR THE WEATHER

31 *July* 2006 ～

Readers of this column in communion with Rome will have noted already that today is the feastday of Ignatius of Loyola. Others not of that persuasion may wish to be reminded that Ignatius was a Spanish soldier who was hit by a cannonball at the siege of Pamplona in 1521; he underwent a spiritual renaissance during his convalescence which culminated in his establishing the Society of Jesus some years later. St Ignatius, as he soon became, died 450 years ago today, on 31 July 1556.

Although primarily concerned with missionary work and education, the Jesuits also channelled their remarkable energies in more mundane directions, and in many parts of the world have been closely associated with the development of modern meteorology. During the nineteenth century, geophysical or astronomical observatories were established at many of their colleges and universities, and at most of these, meteorological observations were also undertaken. By 1930, the Order had more than 30 major meteorological establishments in operation, including observatories in Havana, in Calcutta, La Paz in Bolivia, Ksara in the Lebanon, and San Miguel in Argentina.

The paucity of scientific institutions in these countries, several of them in regions where natural phenomena rarely observed in Europe regularly occurred, made the pioneering work of the Jesuits invaluable, and in many cases they laid the foundations for the future development of a national meteorological infrastructure. Manila Observatory, for example, was founded by the Jesuits in 1865, and in 1884 was designated by the Spanish Government as the headquarters of the Meteorological Service of the Philippines; its mandate was renewed in 1901 by the Americans as the cornerstone of the Philippines Weather Bureau, by which time it was the hub of a regional network of 72 weather stations. Another example was the Jesuit Observatory at Ksara, which was selected as the headquarters of the Syrian Meteorological Service in 1920.

Many individual Jesuits, too, became well-known and loved in their local communities for their meteorological eccentricities. At Santa Clara University in California, Fr Ricard studied the rainfall of the region during the 1920s, and became known as the 'Padre of the Rains'; Fr Benito Vines, Director of Havana

Observatory, who carried out seminal work on tropical revolving storms, was known affectionately as 'the Hurricane Priest'.

From about 1950 onwards, the Jesuits, by and large, took their leave of these meteorological activities in far-flung places. In some cases it was because the rise of national institutions had made their work no longer necessary; in others, like Havana and Shanghai, the coming to power of communist regimes made their tenure less amenable. And in any event, there was by then an emerging view that the proper Jesuit vocation lay, not in observing the idiosyncrasies of the local weather, but in activities with a celestial focus higher still.

A CURIOUS SILENCE IN THE NORTH ATLANTIC

1 *August* 2006 ～

There was a nice little book on the rounds a year or two ago called *The Curious Incident of the Dog in the Night-Time*, written by Mark Haddon. The title, as you may recall, is taken from Sir Arthur Conan Doyle's story *Silver Blaze*, where Watson, responding to Holmes's throwaway remark about just this kind of 'curious incident', says: 'But the dog did nothing in the night-time.' To which the enigmatic Holmes replies: '*That* was the curious incident.'

There have been similarly curious non-events in the Caribbean and the North Atlantic recently. No doubt the dogs are barking normally throughout the region, but, on the other hand, July is over, August has begun, and there have been only two named tropical storms so far this year. Both Alberto in June and Beryl in the middle of July were namby-pamby examples of their ilk, and both expired without reaching hurricane strength. By this time last year—albeit a very exceptional hurricane year indeed—there had been seven storms, with three in July (Cindy, Denis and Emily) becoming full-blown hurricanes.

All this becomes curiouser and curiouser when viewed in the context of announcements earlier this year by the US National Hurricane Centre in Miami that it 'predicts a very active 2006 Atlantic hurricane season'. Pointing out that 'on average, the North Atlantic season produces 11 named storms, with six becoming hurricanes', the Centre went on to say that it expected '13 to 16 named storms in 2006, with eight to 10 becoming hurricanes, of which four to six could become "major" hurricanes of Category 3 or higher'.

But the hurricane season is not over yet. It lasts officially from June until November, both inclusive, and it is mostly in August and September that the killer storms develop; the ides, so to speak, are come but not yet gone. And we can remember 1992, for example—there were no hurricanes at all until mid-August; and then on 24 August Hurricane Andrew hit land in southern Florida, becoming responsible during the following few days for 23 fatalities and damage to property amounting to nearly $30 billion.

In any event, we can be certain that more tropical storms will develop this year to follow Beryl and Alberto. The next is predestined to be called Chris, and a further 18 names have been lined up to serve 2006 when they are needed. These are: Debby, Ernesto and Florence; Gordon, Helene, Isaac and Joyce; Kirk and Leslie; Michael and Nadine; Oscar, Patty and Raphael; and Sandy, Tony, Valerie and William. Should this turn out to be another bumper year like last year—which produced an all-time record of 28 named storms, of which 15 were hurricanes—then, again like last year, the letters of the Greek alphabet will be used to provide labels for the supernumeraries.

OUR LADY OF THE AUGUST SNOW

5 August 2006 ~

S t Ignatius of Loyola, the founder of the Jesuits, whose feast-day was so fervently observed this week in *Weather Eye*, celebrated his first Mass on Christmas Day 1538, in Rome's basilica of Santa Maria Maggiore. So, too, did Fr Eugenio Pacelli in 1899, and forty years later, in 1939, he returned to the church for a Mass of Thanksgiving on his election as Pope Pius XII.

The basilica is one of five in Rome associated with the Pentarchy, the Five Great Sees representing the important fulcrums of the Christian Church in the early Middle Ages. The Patriarch of Rome, the Supreme Pontiff, was, of course, at home; the Patriarchs of Constantinople, Alexandria and Jerusalem had their nominated basilicas in the Holy City, and Santa Maria Maggiore had as its titular incumbent the Patriarch of Antioch.

The basilica, as its title says, is dedicated to the Virgin Mary, and is 'Maggiore' because it excels amongst all the Roman edifices consecrated to her name. Its Pauline chapel contains an icon of the Virgin apocryphally painted from life by no less a personage than Luke the Evangelist himself, and known as *Salus Populi Romani*, the 'Welfare of the Roman People', because of a miracle by which it delivered the citizens from virtual annihilation. According to tradition, it was this icon that Pope St Gregory the Great carried through the streets of Rome in 593 at a time when Rome was threatened with a plague. During this peregrination, St Michael the Archangel appeared to Gregory over Hadrian's Mausoleum, later renamed the Castel Sant'Angelo to commemorate this papal vision; the ephemeral archangel, we are told, drew forth his sword and figuratively warded off the deadly plague, thus saving the city from the epidemic's worst effects.

But it is to another Pope, Liberius, that we owe Santa Maria Maggiore's most intriguing story, and the fact that the basilica itself is sometimes known as Santa Maria della Neve, Our Lady of the Snow. And thereby hangs an interesting tale.

Legend has it that on 4 August 356, the Virgin appeared to Pope Liberius, and told him to build a church on the summit of the Esquiline Hill, an area which at the time was laid out in ornamental gardens. Liberius was informed that the precise location of the church, and the shape that it must take, would be clearly outlined by a fall of snow the following morning. And so it was. The basilica was duly built, and since clearly this snow in early August was miraculous, its occurrence has been commemorated every year since then on 5 August; during a solemn votive Mass in the basilica, a trap-door in the ceiling of the dome is opened to allow a great shower of white rose petals to float down into the nave, thus simulating in perpetuity the Virgin Mary's fall of August snow.

OLD MOORE ON TRIAL

7 August 2006 ∿

Old Moore's Almanac* was first published for the year 1764 by one Theophilus Moore, a Dublin schoolteacher with a flair for the pseudo-science of astrology. At that time many natural phenomena, including the weather, were believed to be associated with the movements of the planets. The Almanac still enjoys a wide circulation every year, and in keeping with its tradition it gives detailed predictions of the character of the weather for the relevant twelve months. Let's see how successful Old Moore has been so far this year.

January 2006, Old Moore declared, would be warmer and sunnier than usual. Fair enough, January turned out to be very mild and dry, and the total hours of sunshine for the month were indeed significantly above the norm. He warned us that there would be heavy snowfalls in the midlands and the north in the first week of February; the south would escape this snow, he predicted, but would experience very heavy rainfall. Alas, *nul points*! There was no snow in February, and the month was mild, dry and relatively sunny. But here it must be said Old Moore was not the only one to get it wrong; some months previously the British Met Office, too, had tentatively predicted very harsh conditions for the close of winter, but they did not come.

The cold weather came instead in March. The first two weeks, according to Old Moore, would be rather colder than usual, and there would be a sudden change to better weather for the remainder of that month. Not bad! The first half of March was indeed very cold, with many showers of snow, but overall it was a rather wet and miserable month.

April, said the seer, would bring its usual showers but nothing too remarkable, and this nondescript weather, he said, would continue into May. April, when it came, was more or less exactly as he said, but May was anything but nondescript; it was, if you recall, the wettest May for twenty years in many parts of Ireland.

Old Moore's June was to be a disappointment: dull and cloudy. In reality it was very pleasant, being sunny, warm and dry. We would have a good July, he said, give or take a thunderstorm or two, and here we cannot fault him; July 2006 was the warmest July on record in some places, and generally warm and sunny.

So far this year, Old Moore's performance has, at best, been mixed. But let us hope that he is right for August. 'You may find yourself wishing you had not booked that foreign holiday,' he says, promising us warm, sunny conditions nearly all the time. Moreover, during the current month, he forecasts, newly released figures will create further worries about the shrinking polar ice caps and lack of action to combat global warming—and that sounds credible enough.

THE MOON IS A LATE RISER

9 *August* 2006 ∿

If there are broken skies tonight, you will see the Moon

> *Full-orbed, and breaking through the scattered clouds,*
> *Shew her broad visage in the crimsoned east.*

It will appear at first as a yellow disc which seems much larger than it ought to be, gradually fading to white as it rises slowly from the horizon towards its zenith.

The Moon's apparent progress westward across the sky results, not from the movement of the Moon itself, but from the *eastward* passage of the surface of the Earth beneath it. In fact the Moon's position relative to the Earth and Sun changes very little in a single night; it is we who move, spinning rapidly on our earthly axis underneath.

Slow as it may be, however, the juxtaposition of the three bodies provides the explanation, not only for the familiar phases of the Moon, but also for the apparently haphazard timetable of its rising and setting. When the Moon is full, as it is at present, it is situated on the opposite side of the Earth from the Sun; for this reason, as the Earth revolves on its axis an observer no sooner sees the Sun set on one horizon than the Moon appears to rise on the one opposite. Their roles are reversed around dawn, with the Moon sinking in the west as the Sun rises again in the east.

Fourteen days later, however, the Moon has moved in its orbit around the Earth into a position directly *between* the Earth and Sun—the 'new Moon' position. Clearly at this point, as viewed from the spinning Earth, the Moon must rise and set *with* the Sun, completing its apparent journey across the sky during the daylight hours—but in these circumstances, of course, we cannot see it.

In between, at other times in the lunar month, there is a gradual transition from one of these extreme situations to the other. During the fourteen days between 'full' and 'new', the Moon has to change from being apparently 12 hours out of step with the Sun to moving across the sky more or less simultaneously with it; it achieves this by rising about 50 minutes later every day (which adds up to 12 hours in the 14-day half-cycle).

After the full Moon tonight, therefore, the Moon will rise almost an hour later each successive night, until by 'last quarter'—

after seven days when it appears as a 'half-Moon'—it will have risen so late that it has time to get only halfway across the sky by the time dawn arrives; conversely, three weeks from now, after the new Moon has passed and the cycle has reached 'first quarter', the half-Moon will be already halfway across the sky when it becomes visible at sunset, and will sink below the western horizon relatively early in the night.

THE PERILS OF UNPOWERED FLIGHT

10 *August* 2006 ◡

It was sad to read in yesterday's *Irish Times* of the death of a veteran aviator in a gliding accident in the vicinity of Kilkenny aerodrome. Ironically, the tragedy occurred 110 years, almost to the day, after the man who began it all, Otto Lilienthal, suffered a similar fate at Stoelln in his native Germany.

Lilienthal was born in 1848 in the Prussian town of Anklam. Throughout his childhood and in early adult years, he recalled, he would gaze for hours at storks and other soaring birds, noting, as it were, the poet William Cowper's conclusion that 'the bird that flutters least is longest on the wing'. From this, Lilienthal concluded that an arched or cambered wing was the most suitable design for flight. He trained to be an engineer, and it was his engineering knowledge applied to ornithology that led him to develop successful designs for heavier than air machines. In 1889 he published his ideas in *Der Vogelflug als Grundlage der*

Fliegekunste—'The Flight of Birds as a Basis for the Art of Flying'—a book acknowledged to this day as a seminal work on aerodynamics.

Lilienthal was the first to think of harnessing the heterogeneous structure of the atmosphere to make sustained flight a real possibility, realising the importance of rising currents of air to sustained unpowered flight. In a static atmosphere, a glider inevitably drifts slowly back to earth; Lilienthal realised that if the aircraft is to *gain* height, it is necessary for the pilot to find areas of the sky where the lift provided by the air is greater than this tendency to sink earthwards—areas with 'thermals', or where the air ascends to clear a ridge of elevated ground. By these insights, Lilienthal laid the foundations which allowed the art of gliding to become the skilful sport it is today.

In 1891 he put his ideas into practice when he built his first man-carrying glider. It consisted of two curved fabric wings to which Lilienthal attached himself by his outstretched arms, and when in the air he used the shifting weight of his hanging body to control the craft, a technique more akin to hang-gliding than to the operation of the more sophisticated gliding aircraft of today. It was the first of many that he built, and using such machines, Lilienthal clocked up more than 2,000 flights throughout his lifetime, reaching heights of over 700 feet.

Lilienthal's magnificent obsession ended tragically when one of his gliders caught a sudden gust of wind, and crashed on this day, 10 August, in 1896. Lilienthal was killed, but his work inspired a new generation of aviators, including the Wright brothers in America, and even today the Lilienthal Medal is one of the highest awards for soaring flight in gliders.

THE CIVIL SERVANT AS A HEAVENLY GUIDE

11 *August* 2006 ∿

Many years ago, when I was a young and keen observer of humanity, my duties required me to interact with civil servants at various levels in different government departments. And in those days life was very, very simple: in the case of male civil servants, you could immediately recognise by the clothes they wore their precise grade and relative position in their hierarchy.

Junior clerical staff, for example, invariably wore jeans. On promotion to Executive Officer, however, jeans were out, and proper trousers and a jumper were preferred. At Assistant Principal level the uniform was a sports-jacket and a pair of slacks, but a suit was *de rigueur* for Principal Officers; it was usually a tweedy green or brown and it could be baggy if the wearer so desired. Darker suits, on the other hand, and always nicely pressed, were the badge of those of Assistant Secretary grade, and pin-stripes, navy blue or black, were the strict preserve of the Department's Secretary General.

All this, to a young man like me, was a reassuring indication that there was a certain order in life's scheme of things. Others, however, have sought their reassurance on a grander scale and tried to find a hierarchical pattern to the arrangement of the universe. Bode's Law seemed to have achieved precisely this in 1766.

Johann Bode pointed out that the sizes of the orbits of the planets could be set down as a series of numbers. The basic series was 3, 6, 12, 24, etc., where each number is its predecessor multiplied by two, but to make the sequence fit the universe, required putting a zero at the start and adding four to each, thus arriving at 4, 7, 10, 16, 28, 52, 100.

The pattern, Bode explained, reflected the proportionate distance of each of the seven known planets from the Sun. If the nearest planet, Mercury, was regarded as being four units distant, then the series accurately predicted that Earth—number three—was 10 units away, and that the outermost planet Saturn was 100 units from the Sun. There was no known planet to fit 28—but otherwise the series was an excellent fit.

The Law was at first a mere mathematical curiosity. But then in 1781 William Herschel discovered Uranus; the next number on the scale was 196, and Uranus turned out to be 190 units from the Sun. And to cement the rule, in 1801 a minor planet, Ceres, was discovered between Mars and Jupiter, and this fitted number 28.

The magic of Bode's Law faded sooner than the dress-code in the civil service. It failed to work for the two outer planets, Neptune and Pluto, and although there is still discussion as to why it should hold good for as many as it does, most astronomers put it down to mere coincidence.

THE DARKER SIDE OF AFRICA

12 *August* 2006 ∾

The weather is a useful tool for novelists. Sunshine conveys an optimistic cheerfulness; a depressing atmosphere is introduced by rain or fog; and windiness has the reader and the characters on edge. And so it is with *The Witchdoctor of Chisale* which I acquired recently on Amazon. Written by a young Dublin doctor, Stephen McWilliams, it is a psychological thriller set in sub-Saharan Africa near the meeting point of Zambia, Zimbabwe and Malawi, and the local climate is central to its *mise en scène*.

The story concerns three Irish medical students who spend their summer vacation helping out at the district hospital in Chisale, Zambia. A sudden and violent death on a mountainside nearby soon interrupts this humdrum exercise in work-experience, and with many twists and turns the plot unfolds in an exciting chase through neighbouring parts of Africa. Their lives are constantly in danger, and over all hovers the malign influence of the enigmatic personage from whom the novel takes its name.

When the action begins, 'the sky was deepest blue, almost navy, while the equatorial Sun pounded down, its burning rays baking the craggy landscape'. But an ambience of uncertainty develops: 'The weather had been worsening all week. It was meant to be getting hotter, drier, calmer—more oppressively so—but instead the winds had picked up with gusts rattling the window panes. The clouds were on the move, occasionally bringing showers, but just as often yielding patches of deep, blue sky.' And as the protagonists climb the Chisale Hills in advance of the climactic tragedy that will transform their world, we find: 'The wind was still blowing relentlessly and showed no signs of abating. The clouds began to look more ominous.'

When the body of the hated Melingu Mwamba is discovered, the elements are restrained in their response: 'The wind had died a little, leaving only a faint rustling in the trees, hushed in recognition of the magnitude of the calamity. The grey clouds were propelled along with less haste, respectfully slowed to a funeral pace.' But when the main protagonist, Robin Carver, has been cleared—for a time, at least—of complicity in Mwamba's death, the weather joins him in celebrating his deliverance: 'Admiring the clear blue sky from where he lay, he soaked up the morning's freshness, its youth, its vitality, its innocence.'

The Witchdoctor of Chisale is a ripping yarn, restrained in tempo while the scene is set, but a classic page-turner as it moves on to its *dénouement*. It is second only to Damon Galgut's *The Good Doctor* in describing the medical challenges in sub-Saharan Africa, and to *King Solomon's Mines* in its ability to grip the reader. But perhaps the most pleasing aspect of the book for this particular reviewer is its dedication. It reads simply: *To my father.*

A WELCOME SPRINKLING OF ANGELS' TEARS

16 *August* 2006 ∿

Rain has come at last. 'Irish rain of the summer and autumn', William Bulfin asserts in *Rambles in Erin*, 'is a kind of damp poem. It is humid fragrance, and it has a way of stealing into your life which disarms anger; it is a soft, apologetic, modest kind of rain.'

After the arrival of the first tentative drop, Bulfin goes on, 'another comes presently, and you feel it on your cheek. Then a few more come. Then the rest of the family encircle you shyly. They are not cold or heavy or splashy. They fall on you as if they were coming from the eyes of many angels weeping for your sins. They caress you rather than pelt you, and they are laden with perfume from the meadow flowers, or the glistening trees, or the sweet, rich earth, or the heathery bogland.'

Well, maybe so. In any event, in my part of the southeast of the country, this has been the first rain of any significance for many, many weeks, and its rejuvenating effect on domestic lawns in the vicinity is almost palpable. The grass has experienced a gradual change in colour recently from emerald green to a parched, deathly yellow, a consequence of what agrometeorologists refer to as a 'soil moisture deficit', or what you and I might think of as simply lack of water.

Of course in areas where official injunctions to conserve supplies do not hold sway, a soil moisture deficit can be repaired by irrigation, but old timers in the gardening world are sometimes heard to mutter that artificial watering is nothing like as effective in promoting growth as William Bulfin's Irish rain.

One major difference between the two is that irrigation is rarely applied in the same external weather conditions as are present when the rain is falling. In wet weather, the atmospheric humidity is at or near 100 per cent, so that evaporation is almost nil; all the applied water is available for absorption by the soil, and therefore, pint for pint, is more effective in promoting growth than water artificially applied in hot, dry, sunny weather.

It is also true that once the soil has dried out, it is difficult at first to persuade it to absorb the added moisture; the water penetrates the surface only very slowly. Natural rain has the advantage that it is applied slowly and evenly over a large area, usually allowing ample time for the parched earth to grow receptive.

But if the hosepipe has a major disadvantage over rain, it often lies in the quality of the water it provides. Rarely will tap-water be as pure as your average raindrop; it may well be that the extraneous substances contained in the former may not be to the taste of some of the thirsty plants to which it is applied.

THE BASIL AND THE BELLS

17 August 2006 ∽

Somewhere in your *Irish Times* yesterday, lost between the multiplicity of Irish murders and the continuing mayhem in the Middle East, you may have seen to your horror that most of the basil crop in northern Italy has been destroyed by hail. The stones which struck in the hinterland of Genoa were reputedly as large as tabletennis balls, and shattered the greenhouses in which the basil plants are grown. The cost of the devastation has been reckoned at four million euro.

Continental hailstorms can be quite different in scale to those we are accustomed to in Ireland. Irish hailstones are typically 'pea-sized'; in southern France, Germany, Austria and northern Italy, however, vigorous thunderstorms frequently produce hail as large as that reported yesterday. A heavy hail-shower typically affects a footprint, or a 'streak', corresponding to the movement of the cloud that bears it; a typical 'hail-streak' might be half a mile in width and five miles long, aligned with the prevailing wind. The large lumps of ice strip leaves from vines, batter crops and cereals to useless pulp, and cause serious damage to cars and fragile structures in their path. In days gone it was not uncommon for a peasant to see a whole year's livelihood swept away within a few minutes.

The accepted wisdom in mediaeval times was that hailstorms were caused by dark spirits in the air. Moreover, the worst of the tribulations might be avoided, it was believed, by frightening away these demons with a loud noise—and what better way to create a din than to ring the church bells as loudly as possible? So ortho-dox was this practice that the Pope authorised a special prayer for use by bishops when consecrating bells: 'Grant, O Lord, that the sound of this bell may drive away harmful storms, hail and strong winds, and that the evil spirits that dwell in the air may by Thy Almighty power be struck to the ground.'

Unfortunately, human nature frustrated these attempts to harness divine acoustic intervention. Firstly, many landowners some distance from the bells believed that the noise diverted hailstones from the vicinity of the church in their direction, and they were understandably annoyed. Another serious problem was the number of bellringers who were killed by lightning, church towers being particularly vulnerable to lightning-strikes. And at the other extreme, some villages complained that they were unfairly treated by the authorities, because they had no bells to ring.

In due course, because of these difficulties, Charlemagne was obliged to issue an edict forbidding the use of church bells for this purpose. But even then, not everyone was satisfied; communities which suffered regular hail damage complained that they were being deprived of the right to defend themselves; many defied the edict, even to the extent of overpowering those unfortunate pastors who tried to implement it.

PLUTO OUSTED FROM THE PREMIERSHIP

18 *August* 2006 ∿

Pluto, you will have heard, must be demoted. If a proposal before the International Astronomical Union is finally approved, the solar system will be deemed to have eight planets, and four of a new category of celestial body to be called *plutons*. Pluto will be relegated to this second division, where it will be joined ignominiously by its own moon Charon, an asteroid called Ceres, and an object named 2003 UB313 after the year in which it was discovered.

The ancients lived comfortably with only five planets in addition to their own: Mercury, Venus, Mars, Jupiter and Saturn. Then in 1781 William Herschel discovered Uranus, but its orbit had a wobble which could be explained only by the gravitational pull of yet another planet in the solar system. In 1846 the French astronomer Le Verrier calculated where it ought to be and a German colleague, Johann Galle, found it as predicted. They called it Neptune.

But Uranus's wobble still seemed to be askew, and the search went on for yet another body; new calculations identified the region of the sky in which to look. In 1929, Clyde Tombaugh, a 24-year-old Kansas high-school graduate with an interest in astronomy was given a job at the Lowell Observatory in Flagstaff, Arizona; in February 1930, he spotted a small 'blink' in the region of the constellation Gemini, and shortly afterwards the observatory unveiled the ninth planet, to be called Pluto.

But there has always been something odd about this new arrival. For one thing, it was a very tiny body compared to its solar system siblings, being only 1,850 miles across and smaller than our earthly Moon. Then in 1978 it was noticed that Pluto had a moon, given the name Charon, which was nearly half as big as Pluto was itself; Pluto, in fact, seemed to be a kind of celestial *pas de deux*.

Moreover, it was soon discovered that the combined mass of the two bodies was insufficient to account for their apparent effect on the orbits of their neighbours. So the mathematicians did their sums again. They found that the apparent discrepancies in the orbit of Uranus were not real, but a consequence of faulty interpretation of the data. It seems that Pluto was discovered quite by accident after all; it was only by lucky chance that it happened at the time to lie in the part of the sky suggested by the calculations.

With such dodgy credentials, it is scarcely surprising that the Pluto ensemble in recent times has come to be viewed with suspicion by astronomers worldwide. After all, the guy who found it wasn't even an astronomer—although he did plough a distinguished furrow later in his life. It comes as no surprise, therefore, that the diminutive duo are to be finally expelled from the inner sanctum of the planetary club.

WHEN IS A PLANET NOT A PLANET?

19 *August* 2006 ∿

'Michael,' says God to the Archangel in Milton's 'Paradise Lost', 'Take to thee from among the Cherubim Thy choice of flaming Warriors,' and

> *Haste thee, and from the Paradise of God*
> *Without remorse drive out the sinful Pair,*
> *From hallowed ground th' unholy, and denounce*
> *To them, and to their Progeny, from thence*
> *Perpetual banishment.*

Astronomers have adopted a similar approach to Pluto and its large moon, Charon, in recommending their banishment from the planetary club. But while Eve and Adam's misdemeanour with the apple is widely accepted as deserving of their punishment, the injunction infringed by Pluto is by no means clear. It revolves, so to speak, around what constitutes a planet in the first place, and no definition, as yet, is universally acceptable.

Some suggest it should be size that matters. Perhaps any body in orbit around the Sun, and greater than, say, 1,000 kilometres across, should automatically qualify, by right of magnitude, to be a planet? This is a beautifully simple concept and coincides with our traditional ideas, but unfortunately it allows in some strange, recently discovered interlopers like 2003 UB313; it would leave us with at least ten planets, and maybe more to come.

Moreover, it is sometimes hard to identify what size a newly discovered distant body actually is. Pluto was originally thought to be much bigger than it has turned out to be; it was gradually down-sized over the years as telescopes improved, to the extent that in 1980 two whimsical astronomers produced a graph which depicted the perceived size of Pluto versus time, and which clearly demonstrated that Pluto would disappear entirely after thirty years.

Another criterion might be the shape of a planetary candidate: perhaps all planets should be spherical? This sets a natural lower qualifying limit because any celestial object above a certain size—about 800 kilometres in diameter—is pulled by gravity into a spheroid shape. It would allow membership to Pluto, but it also admits the asteroid Ceres and at least four other known bodies in the solar system.

Others believe that the term planet should be confined to bodies that dominate their region of the heavens, as nearly all our existing planets do. This criterion rules out the vulgar upstart asteroids, and other far-out bodies that tend to move in swarms—but it excludes Pluto too, which has been accepted as a planet for three-quarters of a century. The contrary view is that we should let tradition rule, keep Pluto, and preserve the celestial usefulness of familiar mnemonics like My Very Energetic Mother Just Served Us Nine Pizzas to remind us of the order of the universe.

But all these criteria have a certain arbitrariness about them—and this, of course, is why it has taken so long to resolve the whole contentious issue in the first place.

THE GASEOUS MONSTER IN THE LAKE

21 *August* 2006 ∽

> *Beware! But hark! what sounds are these?*
> *My dull ears catch no faltering breeze;*
> *No weeping birch nor aspens wake,*
> *Nor breath is dimpling in the lake.*

Twenty years ago exactly, at 9.30pm on 21 August 1986, a mysterious gas rose explosively from the depths of a quiet Africa lake, and killed 1,700 local people almost instantly. Lake Nyos is in Cameroon, a small country just east of Nigeria, under the armpit, so to speak, of western Africa. The gas, it turned out, was a familiar one.

The area surrounding Lake Nyos is volcanic, and it is not uncommon in such regions for volcanic gases to seep through the soil to be wafted away harmlessly by the local winds. In this case, however, large quantities of carbon dioxide ooze upwards into the nether regions of Lake Nyos. In most lakes, this would not be a major problem; winds, cooling the surface waters so that they sink to be replaced by up-welling from below, or the mechanical action of the wind itself, would stir things up sufficiently for the CO_2 to escape, gradually and harmlessly, into the atmosphere above. But things are different at Lake Nyos.

The lake is largely sheltered from such wind as there may be. Moreover, in the tropical heat the surface water is nearly always warmer than water lower down, so there is no mixing. Carbon dioxide accumulating in the bottom layers of the 600-foot-deep lake stays where it is, dissolved by the high pressure of the overlying water into solution with the lowest layers. The whole ensemble resembles a bottle of champagne waiting for the cork to be removed.

No one knows exactly why the lake 'uncorked' in 1986. August is the rainy season, so maybe cool rainwater falling on the surface encouraged mixing; there may have been an unusual pattern of winds; or perhaps a landslide dumped tons of rock into the lake to disturb the delicate balance. In any event the accumulated CO_2 escaped explosively, and once free, and now again in gaseous form because of the reduced pressure, millions of cubic metres of it spread out around the lake. The invisible, suffocating cloud, heavier than air and therefore hugging the contours of the local countryside, killed people and livestock within a range of 25 kilometres.

With the process identified, measures to prevent a recurrence were devised. A pipe was sunk to the bottom of the lake, and once an initial stream of CO_2-rich water had been pumped through it to the surface, the pressure of the dissolved CO_2 below generated a self-sustaining 'soda fountain' to allow the accumulated carbon dioxide to surge upwards through the pipe into the atmosphere in a controlled way. So far, it seems the trick has worked, but ultimately as many as five 'soda fountains' on Lake Nyos may be necessary.

CLIMATIC HERESY ON SUNDAY MORNING

22 *August* 2006 〜

One hears strange things on the radio at times. On *Sunday with Leo Enright* last weekend a contributor told us that the Middle East crisis was getting too much attention on the media. It was 'the non-story of the year', he went on, and 'very few people are genuinely interested. Most people are not affected by it.' This is a situation which has been compared to that of the Balkans in early 1914; and as to its effects—well, we shall see.

Even more startling, however, was a lady on the same show who, during a discussion on the impact of more and more aircraft in the skies on global warming, told us that some scientists 'are saying that if the ozone hole gets any bigger, we are going to need all those aeroplanes to leave that white layer up there to protect us'. I was, as they say in Kerry, knocked out of my standing with the fright of it.

Let us be clear: aeroplanes contribute to global warming, and they have no beneficial impact whatever on the ozone layer. Cheap air travel may have its social and economic benefits, but its effect on the environment is neither positive nor insignificant.

During flight, aircraft engines emit carbon dioxide, oxides of nitrogen, water vapour and tiny particles called aerosols. The enhanced greenhouse effect caused by CO_2 is now accepted and well known, although it must be said that the amount of it in the atmosphere as a direct consequence of aviation is relatively small, comprising about 4 per cent of annual global CO_2 additions to the atmosphere.

Oxides of nitrogen emitted by aircraft flying higher than

16 kilometres contribute, not to the enhancement, but to the depletion of the ozone layer. Aircraft at these altitudes, however, are few and far between. Emitted below about 10 kilometres, oxides of nitrogen do indeed react to form ozone in the upper atmosphere, but ozone generated at this level has no beneficial effect on the fragile ozone layer, which is another 10 kilometres or 20 kilometres higher still; and the ozone hole, which is healing anyway, is a seasonal phenomenon in faraway Antarctica.

Most importantly, however, ozone itself is a very powerful greenhouse gas, and the additional ozone from an aeroplane flight has a warming effect which *exceeds* that of the corresponding CO_2. These two substances, combined with the water vapour emitted by an aircraft—also a greenhouse gas—result in a total contribution to atmospheric warming by an aircraft more than three times that of the CO_2 contribution from the aircraft on its own.

Aerosol particles, the fourth emission, provide the condensation nuclei that allow condensation trails to form. The jury is still out on whether the net effect of contrails is that of an 'umbrella'—causing global cooling—or a 'blanket', contributing to further global warming.

A MACHIAVELLIAN TORNADO

24 *August* 2006 ～

Niccolò Machiavelli was born in Florence in May 1469, and his duties as one of the chief ministers of the republic included missions to all the important courts of Europe, giving him an unrivalled insight into the politics of power. In 1512, however, he fell from favour, and retired to his estates to produce his amoral but influential masterpiece, *The Prince*. It endures as the classic recipe for bad faith and cruelty, and made Machiavelli's name a synonym for duplicity and cunning.

But Machiavelli produced other works as well, including a well-respected tome called *The History of Florence and the Affairs of Italy, from Earliest Times to the Death of Lorenzo the Magnificent*. He gives an interesting account of a violent tempest which raged in the vicinity of Florence 550 years ago today, on 24 August 1456.

Italy at the time was breathing a collective sigh of relief, since the Turks, who had been advancing steadily westwards, had just been soundly defeated at Belgrade. 'In the year 1456,' writes Machiavelli, 'these disturbances having subsided and human weapons laid aside, the heavens seemed to make war against the earth; dreadful tempestuous winds occurred which produced effects unprecedented in Tuscany, and which to posterity will appear marvellous and unaccountable.'

On the twenty-fourth of August, about an hour before daybreak, there arose from the Adriatic near Ancona, a whirlwind, which was accompanied by thick clouds and the most intense and impenetrable darkness, covering a breadth of about two miles in the direction of its course. Under some natural or supernatural influence, this vast and overcharged volume of condensed vapour burst; its fragments contended with indescribable fury, whirling in circles with intense velocity accompanied by winds, impetuous beyond all conception. Flashes of awful brilliancy, and murky, lurid flames incessantly broke forth.

Wherever this awful tempest passed, it produced unprecedented and marvellous effects. Between the castle of St Casciano, about eight miles from Florence, and the Borgo St Andrea upon the same hill, the tempest passed without touching the

latter, and in the former, only threw down some of the battle-
ments and chimneys; but in the space between them, it levelled
many buildings to the ground.

The roofs of the churches of St Martin, at Bagnolo, and Santa
Maria della Pace, were carried more than a mile, unbroken as
when upon their respective edifices. A muleteer and his beasts
were driven from the road into the adjoining valley, and found
dead. All the large oaks and lofty trees which could not bend
beneath its influence, were not only stripped of their branches
but borne a great distance from the places where they grew.
When the tempest had passed over and daylight made the
desolation visible, the inhabitants were transfixed with dismay.

It was, of course, the phenomenon known to us as a tornado.

| COME SEPTEMBER

1 *September* 2006 ∽

L ate last week I awoke one morning to silence in the garden.
All summer long it had been alive with the twittering of
swallows, mainly that of the younger generation vocifer-
ously demanding tribute of their elders, but suddenly, very suddenly, all had disappeared.

The sixteenth-century Archbishop Olaus Magnus of Uppsala
had a theory that at this time of year the swallows descend first
into the reeds, 'and thence into the waters below them, bound
mouth to mouth, wing to wing, and foot to foot,' only to re-emerge

unscathed the following spring. But in our more enlightened times we know that their sudden departure marks the beginning of a five-week, 6,000-mile journey to southern Africa where they will spend the winter. Either way, the vacuum of their silence is a sign of summer's end, and today we have another sign: the calendar announces the arrival of September.

September is the *Introit* to autumn. As we return to school and work, and check the central heating, we recall despondently, particularly with the mediocrity of the last week or two, that 'summer's lease hath all too short a date'. It becomes increasingly obvious that the year is on the turn; its middle age is come and the slow and sad decline into the aches and pains of winter has begun.

Although this month's equinoctial Sun is of equivalent strength to that of March, the early autumn is made softer and more mellow by the lingering warmth of recent summer, and by the still luxuriant foliage upon the trees. September is a month that, by and large, avoids the limelight, lacking the brash exuberance of spring. As Robert Browning put it:

> *Autumn wins you best by this,*
> *Its mute appeal to sympathy for its decay.*

But September can be ambivalent and indecisive. Sometimes it is a windy, blustery month, characterised by a regular procession of depressions moving eastwards across the Atlantic, and passing close to Donegal and Mayo. Occasionally, one of these may harbour the atmospheric remnants of some almost forgotten transatlantic hurricane, as, for example, did the storm we recall as Hurricane Debbie in September 1961. Many of the records for extreme wind speeds established on that day still stand.

But often, too, the march of the Atlantic lows is halted for a time this month by a strategic anticyclone, and one or more spells of fine, dry, quiet weather come along. These, combined with the lengthening nights, encourage the dews and mists we associate with early autumn. September nights are cool, and ground frost becomes a common occurrence as the month matures. The quiet air, cooled by the ground at night, slides down into the valleys and leads to cold 'ponding' in an undulating countryside—a phenomenon often spectacularly in evidence for the home-bound cyclist on a fine September evening.

THE SWALLOWS' AU REVOIR

2 September 2006 ⌒

Those who read this column yesterday will be aware that the swallows who twittered through the summer in my garden have departed for their winter quarters. They have been fun to watch, some days zooming around in their perpetual quest for food within a foot or two of ground level, and on others disporting themselves high in the sky, visible only as tiny dots against the background blue.

There are those who believe that this behaviour gives a clue to future weather: 'swallows high, staying dry; swallows low, wet 'twill blow,' the saying goes. But insofar as there is any truth in this, it is certain that the behaviour of the swallows is dictated by conditions pertaining at the time, rather than by any insight into future weather. These hunters of the air feed while on the wing, and naturally ply their trade in the most bountiful part of the sky at any given time. It is therefore to the distribution of flying insects in the atmosphere that we must look for an explanation of any swallowly behaviour; the birds just go where food is most abundant.

There are two theories on this important issue. The first is that the insects on which swallows prey feel happiest at a barometric pressure of about 1,010 hectopascals; when pressure at ground level is higher than this value—which often happens when the weather is set fair—the insects congregate at a higher altitude than usual. A more plausible explanation, some argue, is that on warm summer days thermal activity carries bubbles of air to heights of many thousands of feet above the ground, and that these rising currents sweep the insects high into the sky. Consequently, on fine days, swallows have to fly progressively higher to maximise their catch of insects.

Be that as it may, the 6,000-mile journey to southern Africa on which our swallows have embarked is a hazardous endeavour. Predators, first of all, are a constant risk. Then those who reach the Mediterranean coast and strike for Africa at Gibraltar are rewarded with a crossing of a mere eight miles, but those that drift out to the west are in danger from the Atlantic's many storms, and thousands collapse exhausted into the sea to die.

The Sahara Desert requires a 900-mile flight which most attempt non-stop, since there will be few, if any, feeding sites *en route*; more birds die on this leg of the journey, apparently, than on any other. The grassy plains of the Sahel provide a bountiful, albeit temporary, respite, but the vast rain forests of the Congo, and more particularly the violent tropical thunderstorms that they attract, take a large toll of the still remaining swallows. Of the five or six offspring of a typical adult pair, only one is likely to survive the journey to return the following year.

STRANGE HAPPENINGS TO THE MOON

7 September 2006 ～

Those of you who believe the Moon is made of green cheese can observe convincing evidence this evening to advance your argument. When the Earth's only satellite rises above the eastern horizon around 8 o'clock, it will be obvious that a large bite has recently been taken out of it; in fact, about 15 per cent of the lunar disc will be missing, and perhaps if you look very closely, you may see a gigantic, gorged, celestial mouse slinking off for his post-prandial cosmic snooze. In any event, the soft, creamy consistency of the green cheese will be confirmed by the fact that over the following half an hour or so, before your very eyes, the Moon will recover to a perfect sphere.

Of course, many astronomers find this evidence of green cheese a little too dilute. They prefer a different explanation; they point to their calculations which suggest that at around 7.42pm this evening, the Harvest Moon, the Earth and the Sun will be in almost a direct straight line. The result, they argue, will be a partial lunar eclipse, at its maximum when the Moon is still below our horizon but still visible when it rises in the east.

When the Sun and the Moon are aligned in space in such a way that Earth is directly in between, it sometimes happens that Earth for a time blocks off the sunlight from the lunar surface. The eclipse that results may be *total*, when the Moon is completely in the shade, or—as will be the case this evening—*partial*, with the Moon just skimming through the outer fringes of the Earth's shadow and only a small portion of it being completely unilluminated.

Unlike an eclipse of the Sun, which is visible only to observers along a relatively short and well-defined local track, a lunar eclipse is visible from anywhere on the dark side of the Earth, provided the Moon is above the horizon at the time. For this reason, although lunar eclipses do not occur as often as their solar counterparts, they are much more commonly observed.

There are two intervals each year, lasting several weeks, when eclipses may occur, and these 'eclipse seasons' slip backwards by about three weeks every calendar year. They currently lie in March and September. In most years there are four eclipses; the maximum possible is seven (four solar and three lunar); while in some years there may be as few as two (both solar). This year, 2006, is nicely average: there was an eclipse of the Moon in mid-March; a solar eclipse visible across Africa and near the Europe-Asia border on 29 March; tonight's event will be the third; and another solar eclipse on 22 September, visible only in the southern hemisphere, will bring the total for the year to four.

COMPLICATIONS OF A HARVEST MOON

8 September 2006 ∿

W hen is Harvest Moon not a Harvest Moon? Clearly the full Moon dominating our night skies at present *ought* to be the Harvest Moon, since it is occurring in September. But there are wingy mysteries and airy subtleties at work; the Harvest Moon, by definition, is the full Moon closest to the autumn equinox, and if you do your calculations very carefully you will discover that the October full Moon on 7 October, which really ought to be 'Hunter's Moon', will be a whisker closer to the equinox, 23 September, than the full Moon which occurred last night.

Whatever you call it, the full Moon at this time of year appears to the casual observer to rise at the same time for several successive nights, almost, as it were, taking over from the Sun. Moonrise throughout the lunar cycle occurs a little later each day by an amount of time known as the *retardation*. The mean value of the retardation is about 50 minutes—but it varies; it is at its maximum of well over an hour around the time of the vernal equinox, and at a minimum around now, in autumn. It was the custom in days gone by for farmers to take advantage of the succession of bright, moonlit evenings to gather in their crops—hence 'Harvest Moon'.

When the full Moon is low in the sky in early evening, as at present, it seems larger than usual. Normally this bigness is just an optical illusion; our perception of its size is influenced by the angular proximity of familiar terrestrial objects, which does not apply when the Moon is near its zenith, and indeed instrumental measurements show that the Moon's angular size is the same whether it is viewed near the horizon or high up in the sky.

But this time the largeness is not entirely illusory. The Moon's orbit around the Earth is not circular, but an ellipse; the distance between the two bodies varies during the monthly cycle by around 30,000 miles. At a certain time in every orbit the Moon is at *perigee*, its nearest point to Earth; perigee is a movable feast within the lunar cycle but this month it coincides with full Moon, which is not only a significant factor in the very high tides that have received attention recently, but also means that the Moon, being closer than usual, appears bigger and brighter than it normally is.

Perhaps this ought to be a cause for some concern, since a proximate Moon was once thought to affect our mental equanimity.

You will recall that in the tragic denouement to *Othello* the distracted Moor detects the baleful influence of perigee: 'It is,' he says,

> *. . . the very error of the Moon;*
> *She comes more near the Earth than she was wont,*
> *And makes men mad.*

| THE SEARCH FOR SEA LEVEL

12 *September* 2006 ∿

Scientists are unanimous in their view that global sea level has been rising for some considerable time, but it is less easy to agree on exactly by how much. Tide gauges at ports around the world have been measuring sea level for decades, and in a few cases for centuries, but unfortunately the land to which these gauges are attached is often moving up and down itself.

Traditionally, the best that could be done was to try to calculate for each site the likely movement up or down of the adjacent land, and then subtract this amount from tide-gauge measurements. In the last decade or so, radar altimeter measurements from satellites have become available; because the position of a spacecraft in space is known precisely, measurements of the vertical distance to the water surface down below allow sea levels to be calculated very accurately indeed.

Changes in the apparent water level at a coastline caused solely by the rise and fall of mean sea level are called *eustatic* changes. Those due to differences in the elevation of the land, on the other hand, are *isostatic* changes and come about in many cases from a delayed reaction to the last Ice Age. Land which has been depressed for centuries by millions of tons of ice tends to rise slowly when the ice retreats, in much the same way as a depressed cork bobs to the surface of a dish of water. And rising land, of course, brings about an apparent fall in coastal water level.

Scandinavia, for example, is still springing back after being crushed by huge glaciers during the last Ice Age, so the sea level around Stockholm appears to be falling at a rate of about four millimetres a year. The eastern seaboard of North America, on the other hand, is slowly sinking, thereby accelerating any rise in the level of the sea that might be evident. Here in Ireland, the ice-cap during the last Ice Age covered only the northern half of the country; in the intervening centuries, therefore, the south coast has been mainly influenced by the eustatic rising trend in global sea level, while in the north this rise has coincided with a similar increase in the elevation of the land, so the net effect on apparent sea level has been very small indeed.

On a global scale, the eustatic rise in sea level between 1870 and 2004 has been estimated at about 20 centimetres, or about 1.5 millimetres per year. The twentieth-century average appears to be around 1.7 mm/year and the rate of rise between 1992 and 2006 has been reckoned as high as 3.2 mm/year. Trends for the future, based on estimates of global warming, suggest a rise in sea level of somewhere between 30 and 80 cm between now and the end of the present century.

| A SYMPHONY IN SAND

13 September 2006 ~

History is silent on King Ozymandias. His name is famous only because of a short poem by Percy Shelley which evokes the futility of human grandeur and the inevitability of ultimate triumph by the elements—in this case by the desert sands:

> *I met a traveller from an antique land*
> *Who said: Two vast and trunkless legs of stone*
> *Stand in the desert. . .*
>
> *And on the pedestal these words appear:*
> *My name is Ozymandias, king of kings:*
> *Look on my works, ye Mighty, and despair!*

The desert always moves. The wind picks up tiny grains of sand and transports them for some distance until they fall to ground again by force of gravity. Where there are obstacles, like Ozymandias's ruined palace, the grains are trapped; the sand accumulates until the obstacle is covered and the way for onward movement of the grains is clear again.

If the wind prevails for long enough, the sand accumulates to form a dune. The dunes themselves migrate under the influence of the wind, and sometimes they produce a form of music, a phenomenon that has come to be known as 'booming dunes'.

Very occasionally, this sound in its most embryonic form can be heard on Irish beaches, when some sands, it seems, 'sing' or 'whistle' when you walk on them. This is known to occur where the tiny grains are dry and very uniform in size, and compared to ordinary sand, the musical grains have surfaces exceptionally smooth. Those who have studied these things tell us that 'this smoothness may be at the heart of the mechanism which transforms the tumbling motion of the grains into very pure oscillations in the air; it prevents the grains from latching on to one another, so that their tendency to dissipate energy soundlessly by sticking together may well be much reduced.'

The dune-booms originate in the 'landslides' or 'avalanches' that are common in very undulating tracts of sand. The mechanism is believed to be the same as that which produces the whistle on the beach, but that the grains of desert sand have a greater variety of size and shape, and therefore provide a richer mix of pitch; the boom, apparently, is the whistle heard *crescendo* combined with the fact that when the sound is heard at a distance, the ear more readily distinguishes the bass components than those of higher pitch—so the sound is perceived as being deep.

The sounds are often loud enough to require people, even in the wilderness, to shout to be heard above the noise. Some dunes emit low, powerful booms; others sound like drumrolls or galloping horses; and some, it is said, are even tuneful. Dune-songs as loud as a low-flying aircraft have been reported on occasion as lasting as long as a quarter of an hour.

REASONS FOR THE SANDY RIBS

14 September 2006 ∽

At the beginning of Samuel Taylor Coleridge's famous epic, according to the helpful commentary, 'an ancient Mariner meeteth three galants bidden to a wedding feast, and detaineth one'. As the scary tale unfolds, the Wedding-Guest becomes uncomfortable, and uses a seaside simile to articulate great unease:

> *I fear thee, ancient Mariner!*
> *I fear thy skinny hand!*
> *And thou art long, and lank, and brown,*
> *As is the ribb'd sea-sand.*

Of course we get his drift; he is alluding to the corrugated pattern of ripples on the surface of a sandy seashore so often evident below high watermark when the tide is low.

The ripples are formed underwater and have been left there by the ebbing tide. Water flowing in and out over the beach by the action of the waves contains little swirls, or eddies, that one might visualise as a kind of mobile version of the hair-curlers used to generate a perm. Each little eddy scoops up a tiny consignment of sand on its formation, and all the eddies die after a more or less common interval of time, abandoning their little hoards of sand on the seabed in a regular pattern which reflects the characteristics of the turbulent flow of the water at the time. When the tide has ebbed, we are left with the familiar ripples.

But even farther up the beach, beyond the immediate influence of the tides, the sand is not entirely smooth. Here the dry, loose accumulation exhibits undulations that are quite different in appearance from the ripples farther down.

These arise from the wind's habit of picking up grains of sand and transporting them for some little distance until they fall to the ground again by the force of gravity. Initially, the surface of even the most undisturbed area of sand will have indentations of some kind, one of which, for the purposes of this exercise, we will imagine as a little valley at right angles to the wind. Airborne grains tending to fall in this vicinity will not land on the sheltered side of this valley, but will rain down on the opposite windward face; in so doing, they tend to push those grains already there up the slope, to create a small hill on the downwind lip of the existing trough.

The process continues. Sand grains on the newly created hill are plucked from the crest by the wind, and being broadly uniform in size and weight, are deposited a common distance downwind, thereby creating yet another little ridge. And so it goes; as the process continues, a state of equilibrium is reached for a given sweep of wind, whereby a series of ripples or ribs will have been created across the entire powdery surface of the sand.

A GLOBAL SUCCESS STORY

16 *September* 2006 ∿

At a time when international squabbles of one kind or another dominate the headlines every day, it is consoling to discover an area of activity where concerted action has achieved success. Since 1995, 16 September has been International Day for the Preservation of the Ozone Layer. The objective of this annual event is to focus popular and media attention on the tribulations of the tenuous veil of ozone that protects our planet from the harmful ultraviolet radiation streaming from the Sun. The date was chosen because it was on 16 September 1987 that the Montreal Protocol was opened for signing, introducing internationally agreed measures to limit the production of the CFC gases and other pollutants that destroy ozone in the stratosphere. It has proved to be a model of its kind.

The problem came to public attention in the early 1980s. The ozone loss was most spectacularly evident in the shape of the annual 'ozone hole' over Antarctica, where regularly each September and October there occurred a 40 to 50 per cent depletion of stratospheric ozone, with the reduction sometimes touching 70 per cent for short periods. Then an average wintertime ozone deficit of around 30 per cent became evident over the Arctic, although the pattern was more erratic and the depletion varied widely from one year to another. Finally, although in the mid-latitudes of both hemispheres the erosion of the ozone layer was less dramatic, it was nonetheless detectable.

The cause was quickly identified to be certain substances, notably industrial pollutants known as CFCs, which facilitated chemical reactions in the high atmosphere that destroyed the ozone. These reactions, by and large, occurred only when temperatures at the relevant levels were much lower than usual, which, together with seasonal wind patterns, explained the variation in the ozone deficit throughout the year.

Unusually, decisive world-wide action involving the great majority of governments was taken very swiftly, and under the Montreal Protocol on Substances that Deplete the Ozone Layer the production of ozone-depleting chemicals was dramatically reduced over a relatively short period. The amount of these substances in the atmosphere has now been declining steadily for over a decade, having reaching a peak in the mid-1990s.

But recovery is slow. There is no *direct* evidence, as yet, of any recovery of the ozone layer itself, and indeed after a comparatively small ozone hole over Antarctica in 2004, last year's hole in 2005 was one of the largest on record. But this is not surprising; it was known that it will take some considerable time for decreasing emissions to translate into increasing amounts of stratospheric ozone. Scientists expect recovery to be clearly detectable from around 2010 onwards, although it will take until about 2050 for the ozone layer to recover to the state it was in a quarter of a century ago.

A MEDITERRANEAN DRENCHING

19 *September* 2006 ∿

That formidable *femme* Lucia, created by the Edwardian novelist E.F. Benson, was of the view that 'it is necessary to *Mediterranizer* oneself every now and then'. This is precisely what *Weather Eye* has been doing for these last few days; we have been oscillating up and down the coast between Montpellier and Perpignan, with the odd sally into the Pyrenean statelet of Andorra.

But oh, *mon Dieu*, the weather! One's meteorological hopes for this region coincide closely with the description given by the writer Tobias Smollett, who lived in Nice for several years in the 1760s: 'Such is the serenity of the air, that you see nothing above your head for several months together but a charming blue expanse, without a cloud or speck; whatever clouds may be formed by evaporation from the sea, they seldom or never hover over this small territory.'

But I should have read my Smollett just a little bit more closely. Later on in the same account he tells us: 'The rainy time is about the autumnal equinox, or rather something later. The heavy rains generally come with a south-west wind which was the *creberque procellis Africus*—Africa, prolific in its storms—of the ancients. It is here called the *Lebeche*, a corruption of *Lybicus*; it rolls the Mediterranean before it in huge waves, and it likewise blows before it all the clouds which have formed above the sea.'

How right he was! It has rained here solidly and uninterruptedly for days, it has been cold and very windy, and in general it has been more like the Kerry Gaeltacht in November than September in the south of France. But both Smollett and the weather map make promise of a better day tomorrow; according to the former: 'These being expended in the rain, fair weather ensues. For this reason the Nisards observe that *le Lebeche raccomode le temps*—the Lebeche repairs the weather.' And the forecasters have promised us a high.

Of course, in general it must be said that the coast of the Mediterranean Sea enjoys one of the most amenable climates in the world. Virtually all its rain falls in the winter half of the year, the summers are dry and almost cloudless, and I am consoled by the fact that the rain, when it does come, tends to fall in relatively short, albeit heavy, episodes. Mediterranean winters, moreover, are very mild, and the summers are hot as well as dry. And the third characteristic of a Mediterranean climate is the great amount of sunshine it implies—well over 2,000 hours a year. The skies are clear and blue for most of the summer, and far less cloudy even in winter than the skies of northern Europe; the week-long palls of cloud, so common in Ireland, are rarely seen in these parts, except, it seems, in the middle of September.

VAN GOGH SURPRISED

22 September 2006 ∾

When Vincent Van Gogh arrived in Arles in the south of France in February 1888, the weather took him somewhat by surprise. He expected, as might we all, sunshine and blue skies; instead, there was snow and ice. And worse was yet to come: 'I have a great deal of trouble painting because of the wind,' he wrote, 'but I pitch my easel into the ground with stakes and go on working; it is too beautiful to stop!'

This fierce wind was the Mistral, a cold, dry, penetrating, parching wind that sweeps down the valley of the Rhone at intervals, most frequently in winter and in early spring. It sends the local populace rushing for cover, waiting behind closed shutters while the raw and dusty menace spends itself. It is noted for the suddenness of its onset, and is most common in the region around Marseilles and Avignon; the town of Arles, as Van Gogh discovered, is directly in its path.

This scourge is an unusual blend—a combination of what meteorologists call a 'fall' wind and a 'ravine' wind. The process starts when large amounts of air cool through contact with the cold mountainside, and slide down to accumulate in the valleys of the French Alps and the Cevennes. There these chilly stagnant reservoirs of air remain, often for some considerable time, waiting to overflow when the right conditions come along. Then a trigger, in the form of a suitable pressure pattern—usually a depression over the Gulf of Genoa and an area of high pressure over central and northern Europe—disturbs these mountain pools, and the result is a flash-flood of cold air cascading down the mountains into the valley of the River Rhone.

The 'ravine' effect is a funnelling of the air which occurs as it is forced to flow southwards along the Rhone valley. Constrictions in this narrow channel result in dramatic increases in the wind speed, and cause the Mistral to be strong, blustery and very often destructive.

Peter Mayle describes the phenomenon very nicely in *A Year in Provence*: 'We had heard stories about the Mistral, how it drives people, and animals, mad. It was an extenuating circumstance in crimes of violence. It blew for fifteen days on end, uprooting trees, overturning cars, smashing windows, tossing elderly ladies into the gutter, splintering telegraph poles, moaning through houses like a cold baleful ghost, causing *la grippe*, domestic squabbles, absenteeism from work, toothache, migraine—every problem in Provence that couldn't be blamed on the politicians was the fault of the *sacre vent*, which the Provencaux spoke about with a kind of masochistic pride.'

Thus the Mistral—and one might surmise that it may have contributed in no small way to the mental problems experienced by Vincent during his second year in Arles.

THE WAVES WERE ALL AGLOW

25 *September* 2006 ∿

Travelling homeward on the *Pont Aven* from Roscoff to Cork over the weekend, I went out on deck somewhere near Land's End to view the ocean, and was reminded immediately of Percy Shelley. The poem that came to mind was

'Stanzas Written in Dejection, near Naples', whose somewhat maudlin atmosphere can be attributed to the fact that not long previously Shelley had been obliged to leave England rather hurriedly, hounded as he was by creditors and troubled by ill-health and social ignominy. And clearly things had not improved since he and his unconventional *ménage* arrived in Italy:

> *Alas! I have nor hope nor health,*
> *Nor peace within, nor calm around . . .*

But it was not Shelley's Neapolitan depression that triggered a reflex in my mind. It was the white foam caused by the ship's passage through the water which was very much whiter than one might have expected it to be by virtue of any illumination coming from the ship itself; moreover the white-capped waves some distance from the boat appeared to switch on and off almost brilliantly like little flashing lights. And I recalled that the dejected Shelley refers to a similar, indeed essentially identical, phenomenon:

> *. . . waves upon the shore,*
> *Like light dissolved in star-showers, thrown . . .*

Both Shelley and I had observed marine *phosphorescence*. This luminous glow emanates from millions of tiny organisms, mostly of the species *Noctiluca miliaris*. The little creatures are about one-fifth of a millimetre in length, and their chemical make-up is such that they emit light when oxygen is dissolved in the water that surrounds them. This happens when the sea is churned up by breaking waves—or by a moving ship, as was the case when I became aware of it.

The phenomenon is more spectacular in the tropical oceans of the world than it is at these latitudes. Passengers aboard a ship in those parts are often treated to a display of an almost continual shower of sparks of light; in the Indian Ocean, in particular, the entire sea is said to seem luminous at times, and a system of enormous bands of light may seem to rotate like the spokes of a wheel across its surface. This phenomenon, sometimes referred to as the 'light wheels of the Indian Ocean', results from the combined optical effects of the phosphorescent bow waves generated by the vessel, the background winds waves, and the motion of the ship itself.

But phosphorescence can be seen close to home as well. It is more frequent in coastal waters than in the middle of the ocean, and indeed it is said that if, on the seashore, you immerse your finger in the sea by day when these phosphorescent creatures are present in great numbers, you may feel a slight prickly sensation, indicating a likelihood that the breaking waves will glow that night.

THE ECCENTRICITY OF THE AVERAGE LOW

27 *September* 2006 ～

S omewhere within the rather untidy complex of low pressure to the west of Ireland this morning lies a mass of warm, moist air which comprises all that remains of what once was Hurricane Helene. But insofar as today's winds may turn out to be unusually vigorous, it is likely that Helene's legacy will have significantly contributed, just as the ghost of Gordon gave us something of a fright a week ago. Despite its pedigree, however, the disturbance to the west is now a normal mid-latitude depression.

The classic depression appears on the weather map as a series of concentric, almost circular, isobars. It corresponds in real life to a great 'bowl' of ever-decreasing pressure, which generates a giant whirlpool of air spiralling anticlockwise towards the centre. Individual examples can be followed on successive weather charts as they move, usually northeastwards, at 30 or 40 mph across the Atlantic, often becoming deeper and more vigorous as they do so. Typically, their path lies close to the northwest coast of Ireland, from where they continue towards Norway, before gradually 'filling up' and dying away.

But depressions do not read the textbooks, and each pursues its destiny in its own particular way. The most obvious deviation from the norm is the path a low may choose to follow. Many proceed impeccably along the track prescribed in the preceding paragraph; but some come farther south, others head north, and the odd maverick may venture where no depression has ever gone before.

Lows are also idiosyncratic in their volatility. The classic example begins as a very small feature, develops into a full-blooded depression over the ocean to the west of Ireland, and then begins to decay. But some may peak perversely prematurely, and be a mere shadow of their former selves by the time they reach our Irish coastline; others are slow developers, and reserve the worst of their fury for regions to the east of us; some die in infancy, while others survive a week or more, expanding in mid-Atlantic to cover the entire ocean and give the weather map the appearance of a dartboard.

And depressions are very often eccentric in a literal sense. If you look closely at a random selection of weather maps, you will see that no depression is exactly symmetrical; the low centre is usually closer to one edge than the other, and as a consequence the isobars on that side are 'squashed' closer together than they are elsewhere. This translates into stronger winds in that vicinity.

Frequently the strongest gales are on the southern side, but sometimes the squeeze is in the northwesterly flow of air behind the low, and at other times in the southerly winds that mark its leading edge. This is the ultimate challenge for the forecaster: that no two depressions are ever quite the same.

THREE KINGS AND TWO WINDS

28 September 2006 ∿

He watched the weather-cock upon the Minster's tower;
First Boreas, blowing from the north, diverted Auster
From the shore, and there were tears of sorrow;
But Auster from the south returned, and he rejoiced.

The sorrowful and then rejoicing watcher of these winds was William, Duke of Normandy, in 1066. The description is that of Guido, Bishop of Amiens, taken from his epic poem *De Bello Hastingensi Carmen*, the 'Song of the Battle of Hastings'. Guido uses the ancient Greek names for the cardinal winds: Boreas for the north wind, and Auster for the south.

The claim of William to the English throne around this time was strongly supported by the Pope, and recruits flocked to his banner from all over France and Germany. The Norman fleet assembled in early August 1066 at the mouth of the River Dive on the northern coast of France, near Caen. But the wind blew steadily from the north, and Norman vessels, having only one rectangular sail, needed an almost following wind for headway; William had to wait—and he was sorrowful. A month later, on 12 September, the wind backed to the west for a time, and William was able to move his ships to St Valery-en-Somme, somewhat closer to his ultimate objective, but there he had to settle down and wait again.

Meanwhile, across the Channel, King Harold of England watched these events with quiet confidence, since he had assembled an army at least as big as William's. But as time went by, with no sign of the invading Normans, Harold had to allow his men to disperse to gather in the harvest. And worse was yet to come; the same northerly wind which proved so troublesome to William provided an ideal opportunity for Hardrada, King of Norway. On 18 September Hardrada sailed his fleet into the Humber estuary, so Harold hurriedly re-combined his harvesters and marched them north to Yorkshire. There on 25 September he decisively defeated Hardrada at Stamford Bridge.

Two days later, however, the wind changed suddenly to southerly. William, as well as rejoicing, lost no time in setting sail for England, and he landed at Pevensey in Sussex on 28 September 1066.

Now, it is arguable that if the northerly wind had lasted for just another week, the course of history might have been entirely different. Harold would have had time to return from Yorkshire to the south of England, and once there, might well have deprived the Normans of their easy landing. In the event, William gained his title 'the Conqueror' by defeating the forces of King Harold near the town of Hastings on 14 October. Poor Harold suffered an arrow through an eye, and was personally disembowelled, beheaded and dismembered by the invading Duke; the subsequent conquest of England was, as we know, equally systematic, ruthless and complete.

THE FERREL EFFECT ON FOOTBALLS

29 September 2006 ∽

The surface of the Earth moves fastest near the equator, where it must complete a circle of 25,000 miles in 24 hours at a speed of just over 1,000 miles per hour. North and south of the equator, however, the surface moves more slowly, since it describes a smaller circle in the course of a day. Approaching the poles, the circle is very small indeed.

The consequences of these different rates of progress for any large-scale movement over the surface of the planet were first outlined by a Frenchman called Gaspard de Coriolis in 1835 and are therefore referred to as the *Coriolis effect*. Coriolis was an engineer by profession, whose main interest was in large turbines and ballistics, and although he was vaguely aware of the implications of his theories for meteorology, he himself did not pay much attention to this application. It was an American meteorologist, William Ferrel, who applied the concept to the wind in 1856; indeed it has often been suggested that in the context of meteorology the phenomenon might more properly be known as the *Ferrel effect*.

The Coriolis effect is a relatively simple concept mathematically, but is difficult to visualise in physical terms. But imagine, for example, an ultrapowerful Derry footballer given a free kick from his home city to a goal in Dungarvan, County Waterford. Looking at the map, it would seem that a shot due south should score. With the Earth moving underneath from west to east, however, a south-bound ball, rather than striking the ground in County Waterford, would land at a point significantly farther west—somewhere, perhaps, in County Cork. To a spectator on the ground, the Derry free would seem to have curved gently to the right.

A similar fate befalls any volume of air moving because of differences in atmospheric pressure. Air flowing from Derry towards Dungarvan will appear to be deflected to the right—just like the football. Conversely, a parcel of air in transit from Waterford towards Derry is moving to a latitude where the surface of the Earth is travelling more slowly; the northbound air will retain its initial eastward momentum, and will also appear to an observer on the ground to have swerved to the right by the time it reaches the latitude of Derry.

All this results in the general rule that air moving over the surface of the Earth in the northern hemisphere is always deflected to the right. It may start to flow directly from high to low pressure, but gradually changes direction until it ends up moving more or less along the isobars with low pressure on its left-hand side. This in turn results in the familiar pattern of the wind in the northern hemisphere blowing in an anticlockwise direction around depressions, and clockwise around anticyclones.

| A MONTH OF CHANGE

2 *October* 2006 ～

October has had many crises of identity. Although originally, as its name implies, it was the eighth month of the old Roman year, late in the first century AD it became *Domitianus.* The change was introduced by the Emperor

Domitian, who was no doubt conscious that his most illustrious predecessors, Augustus and Julius Caesar, had had months named in their honour.

But the new name did not long survive Domitian's death in AD 96. Forty years later, the Emperor Antonius Pius was more subtle; he renamed the month *Faustinus*, after his wife Faustina. And towards the end of the second century AD, October was again renamed *Invictus*, 'the unconquered', this time the allusion being, we are told, to the athletic prowess of the latest emperor, Commodus.

But for most of the past two thousand years, October has been plain October. It retained its name even when it became our tenth month with the reversion of New Year's Day from 1 March to January. In this respect, the Norsemen got it right, calling October *Teomonath*, 'tenth month'. But call it what you will, this month marks a turning of the year, being colder, wetter, darker and windier than its predecessors; as the poet Humbert Wolfe evokes it:

> *Listen! the wind is rising,*
> *And the air is wild with leaves;*
> *We have had our summer evenings:*
> *Now for October eves!*

The temperature on an average October day rises to a mere 13°C or 14°C, three or four degrees less than the September norm. Only very rarely does the temperature exceed 20 degrees, while at the other end of the scale, ground frost occurs on five or six of October's 31 days. Very occasionally, even the air temperature falls below zero—an occurrence almost unheard of in September. The waters around our coasts, too, are becoming colder; the usual sea temperature is around 12°C or 13°C, compared to the August peak of 15 or 16 degrees. And about every ten years or so, a little snow may fall in October, but it tends to melt as soon as it touches ground, and rarely causes trouble.

October is a reminder to us of the rigours of returning winter. There is less Sun than in September, if for no other reason than that the days are significantly shorter; the average September day has some four or five hours of sunshine, while the October average is only three. And yet the month sometimes has a gentler side. Now and then towards the end of October there occurs a spell of quiet, hazy, unseasonably warm weather—a so-called 'Indian Summer', whose spirit is nicely captured by the American writer Henry Adams: 'The Indian Summer of life should be a little sunny and a little sad, and infinite in wealth and depth of tone—just like the season.'

DISASTER ON THE WAY TO INDIA

5 October 2006 ∾

For a brief period in the 1920s and early 1930s, the great airships provided those who could afford it with the ultimate in flying comfort. But a number of tragic and well-publicised disasters, culminating in the *Hindenburg* catastrophe in 1937, turned public opinion strongly against the use of airships, and the lighter-than-air approach to flight was then more or less abandoned. One of the first of this succession of disasters was that of the British *R101* in October 1930.

R101 was dogged by trouble from the start. Throughout extensive trials in the summer of 1930 the engines proved to be very unreliable, and significantly less lift was available than had been predicted on the drawing-board. Moreover, the bags containing the hydrogen, and the outer cover of the framework, both showed an alarming propensity for developing holes; these, we are told, were stitched up as necessary and sealed with rubber solution.

But *R101* had an appointment it was bound to keep. The Secretary of State for Air, Lord Thompson, was due to make a prestigious visit to British India, stopping off *en route* in Cairo, and it was deemed essential that he travel on this latest flagship of the aviation fleet. And so it was that on 4 October 1930, the passengers embarked with their luggage, which in the case of the Secretary of State included a large quantity of champagne, a roll of carpet for the Egyptian King, and a customised Wedgwood dinner service 'lest His Majesty should care to dine on board'.

R101's ill-fated voyage began at Cardington in Bedfordshire, from where the airship headed south for London, and then across the English Channel, making for the Mediterranean coast. At 1.50am on 5 October, the aircraft was near Beauvais, some 50 miles northwest of Paris, and a last message was received by controllers at Le Bourget aerodrome: 'The passengers, having had an excellent meal and having enjoyed a number of cigars, are preparing to retire to bed.' The chief engineer of the airship, who was lucky enough to survive, subsequently described what happened next: 'Just before we arrived over Beauvais we were overtaken by a terrible storm, with squalls of wind and rain and violent whirl-wind eddies. Then suddenly disaster happened. The rain had so wetted the ship that she answered badly to the helm. Twice she dipped dangerously, and then on the third occasion she ran, nose first, into a hill and burst into flames with a very great explosion.'

Within seconds the airship was reduced to a skeleton of twisted steel, and of the 54 people on board, 48 were killed instantly. Those who survived were saved only by a tank of water, which burst above their heads and protected them from the inferno by drenching them with water.

THE MYSTERIOUS AFFAIRS
OF STATE

10 *October* 2006 ∿

Hermes Trismegistus was a psychopomp. This is no aspersion on either his personal demeanour or his mental health; it is a job description. It tells us that 'Thrice-Greatest' Hermes, as his name translates, was one of those minor deities of ancient times whose duties included the guiding of dead souls safely into the regions of the afterlife. But Hermes is also regarded as the *fons et origo* of the mysterious pseudo-science of alchemy. We still unwittingly use his name from time to time when we speak of an 'hermetic' seal; Hermes, apparently, made very sure that his secrets did not leak, and his knowledge of the divine art was handed down from father to son only through the royal line of ancient Egypt.

The alchemists believed that there was ultimately only one elemental matter, and that every substance in the world could be reduced to this. As a sideline in their search for this *materia prima*, mediaeval experimenters spent much time trying to discover the panacean *elixir vitae* and the philosopher's stone which they believed had the capability of transforming baser metals into gold. Meteorologists, of course, have long since abandoned alchemy as a *modus operandi* of their trade, but they observe with great interest the transformations of water from one state to another with a change in temperature, transformations which account for nearly all the weather phenomena that affect us every day. Water might be described as the *materia prima* of the weather.

Water exists in three phases: solid, liquid and water vapour. With three phases, six transformations are possible, and each of them occurs in nature. The change from solid to liquid, for example, is called *melting*, and the change from liquid to solid is the familiar process of *freezing*. Liquid transforms into water vapour by *evaporation*—as when the puddles left by a shower of rain quickly disappear. And the reverse process, a change from vapour to liquid, is the familiar *condensation*; we see it in action on window-panes when warm, moist air inside a room is cooled by contact with the cold glass, and it also accounts for the formation of many clouds and most varieties of fog.

The two remaining transformations are less obvious; in both cases nature skips a step, and the process is known as *sublimation*. If the temperature is low enough, dry air trying to absorb water vapour will sometimes snatch it directly from a surface of ice; the ice, in a sense, evaporates directly into thin air. And in the opposite direction, also in very cold conditions, water vapour may 'condense' directly into ice; this is the process of *deposition*, whereby the tiny ice crystals of very cold clouds are formed, and in a more familiar setting it accounts for 'hoar frost', the white crystalline deposit which is the characteristic trade-mark of a cold and frosty winter's morning.

AN ECCENTRIC BORN BEFORE HIS TIME

11 *October* 2006 ✒

Lewis Fry Richardson was born into a well-known Quaker family of the north of England. As his middle name recalls, he was distantly related to certain successful manufacturers of chocolate, and his nephew, Sir Ralph Richardson, was to become one of the foremost actors his time. But of Lewis Fry Richardson himself, born 125 years ago today on 11 October 1881, very few have heard.

Young Lewis grew up to be the archetypal nutty professor of the storybooks. One of his last scientific papers, for example, begins with an unforgettable announcement: 'We have observed the relative motion of two floating pieces of parsnip . . .'. Another examines the analogy between sparks and mental images, in an attempt to explain the phenomenon of sudden thoughts or 'brain-waves'. And shortly after the *Titanic* sank, Richardson with an umbrella was observed blowing a penny whistle in a rowing boat; he was using the umbrella both as an amplifier and a receiver to gauge the strength of the sound reflected from the nearby cliffs, thus anticipating the apparatus that we now call SONAR.

Richardson's most far-fetched notion at the time, however, was that a weather forecast might be produced by calculation. Building on the theories of the Norwegian meteorologist Vilhelm Bjerknes, Richardson had the idea that the future pressure pattern could be calculated if the present state of the atmosphere were accurately known. He proposed using a number of equations which encapsulated many of the known principles of physics, like Boyle's Law and Newton's Laws of Motion, and these would be applied repeatedly to advance the forecast in very short time-steps. The theory seemed plausible, but it involved an inordinate amount of calculation.

Undaunted, Richardson tried out his methodology. During World War I, he worked as an ambulance driver in the Champagne district of northeastern France just behind the Western front, and it was in these extraordinary conditions, in 1917, that he carried out one of the most remarkable computational feats ever to be accomplished. Using as his starting point a selection of weather observations from over western Europe for 7am on 20 May 1910, he painstakingly worked through the necessary calculations, taking several months to produce a six-hour forecast.

He published his results in 1922 in *Weather Prediction by Numerical Process*, a book that has become one of the classic works of meteorology. But they were disappointing. Richardson's forecast predicted pressure changes of up to 150 hectopascals in the six-hour period, a totally unrealistic figure.

As it turned out, however, Richardson was merely a prophet born before his time. The arrival of the electronic computer in the early 1950s changed the scene dramatically. Richardson's methods were vindicated, his methodology was improved, and 'numerical weather prediction', as we call it now, became reality. By the 1990s, it had become the standard method for producing weather forecasts.

A DAY IN HONOUR OF THE ASH

12 *October* 2006 ∾

D id you know that it requires half a million hurleys every year to replenish the national stock of these uniquely Irish sporting implements? This remarkable statistic was unveiled recently by the Tree Council of Ireland in its lead-up to Tree Day 2005—which is today. On Tree Day every year, primary schools throughout the country put aside their fixation with reading, writing and arithmetic and focus instead on forestry and trees. In this context, 2005 has been designated 'The Year of the Ash'.

Now, ten thousand years ago there were no trees at all in Ireland. Ice covered all of Scandinavia, part of Ireland and a large tract of North America; modern France and Germany were reduced to a state of permafrost and the familiar species of trees survived only in little pockets of what we would now call a 'temperate' climate on the Mediterranean peninsulas, those of Italy, the Balkans and Iberia. Then, as the ice retreated, the trees began the slow process of re-population; birches and willows gradually re-gained a foothold, followed later by alder and pine, the oak and elm, and along with them, the ash. It is now wide-spread in Ireland but grows particularly well in counties Tipperary, Meath, and Kildare; Cork, Clare and Kilkenny; and Waterford and Galway. It thrives best in lowland areas compara-tively free of frost.

Strangely enough, ash is one of the trees more vulnerable to lightning strikes. Trees vary in their moisture content, and those high on the scale in this respect offer an easier path to earth for the electric currents that constitute a lightning strike. Surveys tell us that the oak tree is by far the most susceptible target, accounting for some 35 per cent of lightning strikes on trees; elm is next at around 20 per cent, and ash follows closely behind in terms of vul-nerability. Folklore confirms the general thrust of these statistics:

> *Beware of the oak—it draws the stroke;*
> *Avoid an ash—it courts the flash;*
> *Creep under the thorn—it'll save you from harm.*

Folklore also gives the ash a part to play in weather prediction. Every spring our ancestors would watch the relative progress of the oak and the ash with great interest, and the order of their coming into bud was seen as an infallible rainfall indicator for the future harvest:

If buds the ash before the oak,
You'll surely have a summer soak;
But if behind the oak the ash is,
You'll only have a few light splashes.

And another feature of the ash brings us back again to hurleys. The timber of the ash, apparently, possesses a highly desirable combination of flexibility and strength, which makes it the ideal material, not only for hurleys, but also for oars and for the handles of a wide variety of tools.

NEGATIVE FEELINGS— POSITIVE CAUSES AND *VICE VERSA*

20 *October* 2006 ∿

Poor Hamlet gets very dejected around the middle of Act 11. 'I have of late,' he says, 'but wherefore I know not, lost all my mirth, foregone all custom of exercises.' His depression, of course, may well have been a reaction to his own procrastination or some mediaeval version of ME, but it might also be that the Danish air was rich in positive ions at the time, those tiny electrically-charged particles that some scientists believe can adversely affect our physical and mental wellbeing. Hamlet himself, indeed, hints at such a possibility: 'This most excellent canopy, the air . . . this brave o'erhanging firmament, . . . appeareth nothing to me but a foul and pestilent congregation of vapours.'

Molecules of air comprise atoms in many combinations. Atoms, moreover, contain a number of tiny, negatively-charged particles called electrons, and these electrons are incurably promiscuous; at the slightest stimulus an electron will abandon its atomic home and the molecular family to which it properly belongs.

As in real life, this departure brings a sense of loss. The molecule, deprived of some of its negative charge, is no longer electrically neutral, and is left holding a net positive charge; we now call it a *positive ion*. But the errant electron soon finds a new home; it attaches itself to some adjacent molecule, which then has a surfeit of negative charge, and becomes a *negative ion*.

Now, the reason we bother ourselves with these vagrant, minuscule dots of electricity is that there is evidence to suggest that ions may affect our wellbeing. Most of the time, negative and positive ions are present in the air in roughly equal quantities, but sometimes one or the other may predominate. The air becomes rich in positive ions, for example, during a thunderstorm, and in the vicinity of fire. It is said that a preponderance of positive ions produces irritability and anxiety in a susceptible 30 per cent of the population, and may even induce physical symptoms like nausea and headaches. It is alleged that the Mistral wind of southern France, the Santa Ana which blows in California, and Italy's Sirocco wind are all laden with positive ions, and that this accounts for the unpleasant psychological effects that they are known to bring about.

Negative ions, on the other hand, are said to induce a sense of physical and mental wellbeing. There is normally a high concentration of negative ions near the seashore and in the rarefied air at the summits of high mountains; negative ions are also present in abundance in the vicinity of waterfalls, created by the breaking up of water droplets into a fine spray. By the same process, negative ions are created in the domestic shower, and this, we are told, is the reason why a shower produces a feeling of freshness and invigoration superior to the traditional bath.

INDEX